I0037311

SWIPE RIGHT

ON YOUR

BEST SELF

ERIC WINTERS

WHAT OTHERS SAY

Well-written, entertaining, and based on solid science, this book will give you effective and practical strategies to be who you really want to be and do what you really want to do. A playful and practical approach to building the life you want, and handling all the stress that goes with it.

Russ Harris, author of the international bestseller *The Happiness Trap*

I love *Swipe Right on Your Best Self*. It is the three things that any great personal development book should be: diligently researched and referenced; clear and eminently practical; and wonderfully entertaining and inspiring.

Eric draws on an incredibly broad range of theories and approaches to make a compelling diagnosis of the stuff in ourselves and our culture that keeps us stuck – and to provide a comprehensive plan for how we can get ourselves unstuck and living life on our own terms.

Eric is a great storyteller. Every chapter uses examples from his own life and from history to bring potentially complex theories clearly into focus. The language is clear and accessible, and it is a dream to read.

This is a book I will recommend to friends, colleagues and clients, and one that I will read and re-read myself.

Jon Hill, Director of Blueprint Coaching and Training, co-author of *Acceptance and Commitment Coaching*

Eric Winters has a certain charm in how he articulates psychological science and that charm oozes the whole way through this incredibly powerful and accessible book! Well done Eric on pulling together ribbons of scientific strategies to weave a beautifully colourful and vital piece of information which is simultaneously a pure joy to read!

Dr Suzy Green, CEO of The Positivity Institute and author of *The Positivity Prescription*

Eric has created an inspiring roadmap to achieving our best authentic self through courage, the courage to choose a path in life full of meaning, gratitude and humanity. His metaphor of authoring our own lives enables us to think more clearly about how we can write a new page each day if yesterday's version did not hit the mark. Eric uses his own story, including his vulnerabilities and successes, which gives his 'Swipe Right' model gravitas. He uses humour in an engaging way, which strikes to the very heart of his message – live life to the max with no regrets! *Swipe Right on Your Best Self* is a simple but intellectual guide to investing in, and finding, your best self!

Jennifer Wittwer, CSM, FAHRI, Thought leader, gender champion, UN consultant and author of *Against the Wind: How women can be their authentic selves in male-dominated professions*

A fun, fast-paced book about developing courage. Eric has brought together a broad range of seemingly complex evidence-based coaching psychology concepts into a set of easy-to-read chapters. Each chapter ends with a summary which builds into a seven-step guide to developing the best version of your courageous self. Applying the leadership lens, courage is an essential ingredient to collaborating and adapting during challenging times. Our leaders could all benefit from these simple evidence-based steps and practices. Congratulations to Eric for bringing such diverse ideas together into an engaging and practical guide.

James Farrell, Financial Services Industry Executive, Microsoft

I love that a well-lived life is a risky adventure, and this book is a guide and coaching tool through this journey to help us show up authentically and courageously. Rather than just white-knuckling it through the challenges of life this book provides a series of strategies to think, feel and move through challenges in a proactive and productive manner. Living an awesome life doesn't just happen by chance, and Eric guides the reader beautifully with strategies that can be easily adopted to live a more courageous, authentic life and most importantly put the reader in the driver's seat. I thoroughly enjoyed reading this book. The easy-to-implement framework to understand my challenges and how to lean into them is something I'm implementing in my personal and professional life. This is something I believe everyone should implement. Congratulations on an amazing book!

Ally Muller, Innovation leader and Founder of Goya Consulting

There is a lot that I love in Eric Winters' new book, *Swipe Right on Your Best Self*. The more I read, the more I felt the rising and often overwhelming desire to embrace the concept of courageous authenticity. A mighty thought delivered beautifully in this powerful and deeply considered book that is part autobiography and part self-development, blended perfectly with a very solid dose of worldly wisdom. If you want to live a bolder life, with fewer regrets (and let's be honest, who doesn't?), this book will help you achieve this. A very heartfelt congratulations, Eric.

Andrew Griffiths, International Bestselling Business Author, Global Entrepreneurial Speaker

Eric Winters is a delightful human being. A talented and emotionally generous coach, author and speaker, he brings a unique approach to creating positive change. In *Swipe Right on Your Best Self*, Eric presents some of the best science available to help us reflect, reset and redirect our lives towards greater satisfaction. Of particular value is the summarising framework 'swipe right in seven steps', which connects different areas of our knowledge on living well. It's an illuminating gift as it feels like you have just been given a peak behind the magician's curtain. The seven steps will show you how to take action now and reap the benefits now, and how to repeat that in an ongoing way.

From the moment you open this book, you have met a new friend, a friend who will gently show you how to feel and do better. I highly recommend *Swipe Right on Your Best Self*, a book just right for this moment in history when individually and collectively we need to reflect and reset, orientating more closely to what is truly important in life for ourselves, our loved ones and our planet.

Thank you, Eric.

Dr Elizabeth King, Coaching Psychology Unit, University of Sydney

I loved this book! The thoughtful self-reflection which lies at the heart of Eric Winters' *Swipe Right on Your Best Self* is a process of immersion in an engaging, intimate and nourishing dialogue; akin to an absorbing conversation with an old friend, who is both witty and wise. A friend who also understands the wit and wisdom in you. A friend who brings out the best in you because – as you will discern from turning these pages – the best of you is what he sees. Wholeheartedly recommended!

David Rankin, Financial Coach and Founder of Sort My Money

This book is packed full of wise and important advice, all delivered with warmth and good humour. Eric doesn't pretend to be the perfect person who has all the answers, but is willing to be authentic and vulnerable, someone who, like me (and perhaps you?) struggles and fails and returns over and over again on a path of self-care and compassion. I love his honesty. I highly recommend this lovely book.

Rachel Collis, author of *Applying Acceptance and Commitment Training to Work-Related Coaching*, co-author of the Working with ACT blog, Executive and Leadership Coach, Sessional Academic at Queensland University of Technology, Graduate School of Business

Vulnerable and refreshingly honest, *Swipe Right on Your Best Self* integrates a broad range of evidence-based concepts and makes them accessible to people from all walks of life – equally applicable to corporate and community. Within organisations, understanding and acting on this knowledge to support personal growth and wellbeing is no longer negotiable but essential to cope with the fast-paced, complex and uncertain world we live in. Eric's authentic writing style challenges your thinking while making you smile, and provides the perfect handbook to dip in and out. The 'Swipe Right' model holds a mirror to what is holding you back and provides practical techniques to move forward. This is a book I would definitely recommend for anyone who is focused on developing themselves or others to help them not only survive but thrive.

Claire McCaffery, Talent and Leadership, Accenture

Hats off to Eric – awesome work! This is an accessible, practical and fun book – firmly grounded in evidence-based behavioural science. Eric takes the reader on an engaging and compelling journey that brings together threads from history, fiction, pop and his personal experience to illustrate each stage of his relatable proposition. He is an outstanding guide to the human condition and helping us all realise that 'taking courageous action is an ability, a skill to develop.' Let's get out there and spread the science.

Ross McIntosh, Organisational and Coaching Psychologist, UK Government Internal Audit Agency and host of the People Soup podcast

ACKNOWLEDGEMENTS

In September 2019 I met an angel.

I was deep in the Jamison Valley in the Blue Mountains National Park, sitting uncomfortably on the forest floor when the leaves began to tremble. The air throbbed, softly at first, and then hummed in anticipation. Tree branches above swayed then respectfully parted to reveal an athletic female figure descending between them. She stepped lightly upon the earth and strode over. Kneeling beside me she said, 'Hi, I'm Libby. Tell me what happened.'

I'd broken my leg three hours earlier and couldn't stand. Embarrassingly, I hadn't been abseiling, climbing or canyoning – all story-worthy ways of damaging yourself. No, I'd been merely hiking along a popular valley path when I'd tripped and fallen among some small boulders. My 55-year-old shinbone collided with a 250-million-year-old rock.

With reassuring professionalism, my paramedic Libby took charge of the situation and clipped me to her wings. We ascended together into the rescue helicopter hovering loudly above. It had taken two-and-a-half hours to drive to the start of the hike but just 20 thrilling minutes to fly back to my local hospital. We landed on the roof to be greeted by a bouquet of attentive pastel-clad medics. M*A*S*H without the music.

I recall being wheeled into surgery, but cannot remember being given the anaesthetic which swept me into oblivion. Skilful hands submerged my consciousness for five hours before hauling my torpid mind and repaired frame to the surface again. There's so much metal work inside now that I've named my enhanced limb RoboLeg. The quality of nursing and medical care I received in hospital over the next week was fantastic – professional, generous and compassionate. I then spent the next three months on my back at home, my angry right tibia grumbling as it knitted new bone across an extensive spiral fracture.

I had been meaning to write this book much sooner, but couldn't seem to find the time. My calendar had been a multi-coloured patchwork of the work I love most: developing bold leadership through keynotes, workshops and coaching, across Australia, China and Papua New Guinea. The Roman goddess Fortuna had glanced at all this, smiled wryly, and nudged my fragile human body into enduring ancient rock. In an instant, all calendar commitments for the next 90 days were cleared.

No more excuses. It was time to start writing.

So, I'd like to begin this book by thanking those who helped make it possible. Thank you Fortuna, Libby the NSW paramedic, the Toll Ambulance Rescue Helicopter Service, my surgeon Edward O'Leary, and the extensive team of compassionate and skilled nurses, doctors and physiotherapists who have taken such good care of me. Even Joanna, the east-European blood-taking nurse with the suspiciously vampiric accent, thank you. You were all incredible.

And special thanks to my partner Rachel, who was such a kind, willing and generous carer while I was out of order for so long.

This book represents a harvest of ideas gathered from many talented thinkers, teachers, researchers, practitioners, philosophers and writers. I've been especially privileged to learn directly from thought leaders in behavioural science, positive psychology, emotional intelligence and coaching in Australia, the US and the UK. So in no particular order (and cruelly leaving many others out), thank you Alain de Botton,

ACKNOWLEDGEMENTS

Tony Grant, Steven Hayes, Niklas Törneke, Russ Harris, Kevin Polk, Benjamin Schoendorff, Rick Hanson, Robert Kegan, Lisa Lahey, Barbara Frederickson and Kristin Neff – your workshops and lectures were transformative. I've taken your ideas, mangled them and misrepresented them. You may not recognise them. But thank you.

I'm also grateful to the writers whose names appear throughout this book and at the end of each chapter. Your ideas have been invaluable.

Thank you everyone.

Eric Winters

First published in 2020 by Eric Winters

© 2020 Eric Winters
The moral rights of the author have been asserted

Back cover quote is from *The Top Five Regrets of the Dying: A life transformed by the dearly departing*, by Bronnie Ware

All rights reserved. Except as permitted under the *Australian Copyright Act 1968* (for example, a fair dealing for the purposes of study, research, criticism or review), no part of this book may be reproduced, stored in a retrieval system, communicated or transmitted in any form or by any means without prior written permission.

All inquiries should be made to the author.

A catalogue entry for this book is available from the National Library of Australia.

ISBN: 978-1-925921-96-0

Project management and text design by Michael Hanrahan Publishing
Cover design by Peter Reardon

Image page 16 by acrogame from Adobe Stock.

Image page 26: This image has been identified as being free of known restrictions under copyright law, including all related and neighboring rights.

Disclaimer

The material in this publication is of the nature of general comment only, and does not represent professional advice. It is not intended to provide specific guidance for particular circumstances and it should not be relied on as the basis for any decision to take action or not take action on any matter which it covers. Readers should obtain professional advice where appropriate, before making any such decision. To the maximum extent permitted by law, the author and publisher disclaim all responsibility and liability to any person, arising directly or indirectly from any person taking or not taking action based on the information in this publication.

CONTENTS

COURAGE IN THE TIME OF CORONAVIRUS

As I wrote the closing chapters of this book in 2019, a single individual in Wuhan, the most populous city in Central China, became infected with a coronavirus entirely new to human biology. With neither natural immunity nor a vaccine to slow its spread, the virus has exploded across human populations globally. The COVID-19 pandemic has momentum. It has reminded us that we are all more interconnected, interdependent and fragile than we had realised.

The global challenge has revealed the entire spectrum of human responses. The reactive, self-interested and avoidant, through to the proactive, prosocial and courageous.

This book is dedicated to the courageous. To all those who have put the needs of others ahead of their own. To those who have done what was right, but difficult. To those who have risked their health, their careers, their everything.

Conspicuous examples of courageous leadership include:

- Dr Li Wenliang, the Chinese doctor working at Wuhan Central Hospital who first noticed an outbreak of a SARS-like virus and warned fellow doctors to wear protective clothing. He was silenced by the Public Security Bureau who accused him of 'severely disturbing the social order'. Dr Li Wenliang subsequently became infected with COVID-19, contracted while treating patients, and died.

- Captain Brett Crozier of the USS Theodore Roosevelt, fired for daring to plead to his superiors for help with a coronavirus outbreak among his crew.

- New Zealand Prime Minister Jacinda Adern, who provided Western leaders with a masterclass in leadership that combines courage, compassion and clarity. She's been on the front foot in implementing measures to contain the virus, and at the time of writing New Zealand is the only country with the bold goal of eliminating the virus from its shores.

However, most acts of courage do not make the news. This book is dedicated to all those who have responded to the COVID-19 challenge with quiet and inconspicuous courage:

- To all those who have taken care of others by stepping forward when people needed them. Health workers are especially thanked.

- To those who have taken care of others by stepping back. By keeping their distance. By staying at home. Often the most courageous thing any of us can do in life is to demonstrate restraint. Thank you.

This book was finished before 30 January 2020, the day the World Health Organization declared a Public Health Emergency of International Concern. The following pages do not mention coronavirus, COVID-19 nor the disease it causes, SARS-CoV-2. However, the importance of developing courage to meet life's challenges effectively is obviously more relevant now than ever before.

This book is dedicated to those who have shown us humanity at its best.

INTRODUCTION

'A man with outward courage dares to die;
a man with inner courage dares to live.'

LAO TZU

SWIPING RIGHT ON OTHERS

Tinder.

It sounded like an online supermarket for hook-ups. With my mind uncontaminated by experience but informed by salacious media, I fantasised about wandering down virtual aisles of women. Or did I sit on the shelf and they were doing the browsing?

I never expected to visit the Tinderverse. I'd been in a meaningful long-term relationship for many years. We were happily committed to one another. I thought. Then one evening, with no warning at all, my partner told me she'd been seeing an old flame – for some time. Not only seeing him, of course. After test driving, she had decided to trade me in. I was incredulous, then devastated. The person I'd trusted most in life was untrustworthy.

Could anyone be trusted? Could I be certain of anything?[1]

I grieved, processed, and eventually recovered the equilibrium I'd lost. Ultimately I was ready to consider another relationship. Online dating had now become mainstream, a routine approach to meeting potential partners for people of all ages. After a little research, I discovered my initial assessment of Tinder had been largely fantasy. Casual sex appeared to be a minority interest, Tinderland being mostly populated by people looking for something more enduring. Tinder also had considerable competition, from similar apps such as Bumble and OkCupid. Whatever you are looking for, there's an app for that.

As you may already know, dating apps tend to work along similar lines. You usually create a profile with a brief description of yourself, one or more photos, your age, location and preferred age range for a date. Then you press the search button. The process is less like wandering down supermarket aisles and more like sitting beside a sushi train. Possible choices arrive one at a time. Like what you see? Swipe right, as many times as you like. Not interested? Swipe left. If both parties are interested, it's a match! You can message one another and take it from there.

Would getting a great date really be as easy as ordering a customised pizza online? I decided to find out.

No. It would not.

I could get dates, sure, but mostly with people who weren't right for me. At all. I embarked on a steep learning curve.

---

1 If you've been touched by the profoundly destructive pain of betrayal, do read Esther Perel's fabulous *The State of Affairs: Rethinking infidelity*. It's a compassionate exploration into many surprising causes and life-changing consequences of infidelity. There was consolation and insight within the pages. Five stars. And if you're considering infidelity, I heartily recommend reading this first. Always worth making an informed decision, don't you think?

Everything changed as I got better at doing three things. Then I started meeting more and more wonderful, funny, smart, attractive and increasingly appealing women. I'm not saying this will help anyone else, but here are the three steps I took that made all the difference:

1. **Knowing.** First I got more honest with myself. What *really* mattered to me? What kind of a person was I, and what did I care about? What was a bit odd or challenging about me? What sort of qualities was I looking for? What were the behaviours I appreciated in others? What were the deal breakers? I made a fearless inventory.

2. **Naming.** I then described myself and my preferred partner in full, honest, unvarnished and vulnerable detail. I did my best to be courageously authentic. This helped unsuitable dates to reject me. It helped great matches to recognise me.

3. **Noticing.** As Maya Angelou wrote: 'When someone shows you who they are, believe them the first time.' People reveal themselves with everything they write, say and do. I paid more attention. I believed them. I moved away from mismatches and moved towards good matches.

That was it.

Suddenly I was spending more time with people whose company was energising and nourishing rather than draining and disappointing. Ultimately I met someone extraordinary. We're still together, still doing our best to show up authentically to each other every day. If you are going to be in an intimate relationship, it's worth choosing carefully – there's a lot at stake, after all.

However, there's someone else whose identity will have an even bigger impact on your energy, wellbeing and quality of life …

SWIPING RIGHT ON YOUR BEST SELF

There's a lot in life that's not in our control. We don't get to choose our genes, our parents, how we were brought up, the schools we went to or the culture we grew up in.

It's been said that acceptance means giving up hope of a better past. Fair enough. However, acceptance also includes taking ownership of our present, and the opportunities and choices we make from here on. Whatever our circumstances, we get to choose how we show up each day. Our attitudes and priorities, how we treat others and ourselves – that's up to us. As Holocaust survivor Viktor Frankl wrote in *Man's Search for Meaning*: 'Everything can be taken from a man but one thing: the last of the human freedoms – to choose one's attitude in any given set of circumstances, to choose one's own way.' Frankl wrote his book after surviving internment in four Nazi concentration camps, including the horrific Auschwitz extermination camp. The original title of his book was *Nevertheless, Say Yes To Life*.

The top regret of the dying

Each of us chooses *how* we say yes to life each day. We choose what kind of self we swipe right on. The dying have some profound wisdom to share on the subject.

Bronnie Ware spent years working as a palliative care nurse in Australia, taking care of hundreds of people during their last weeks or months. People would share brutally honest personal reflections on their lives and regrets. Bronnie noticed that although all life stories were unique, there were some regrets that showed up again and again. She describes these in her moving book *The Top Five Regrets of the Dying*.

The book you are reading now focuses on avoiding the biggest regret of them all:

I wish I'd had the courage to live a life true to myself, not the life others expected of me.

The regrets voiced by the dying are precious gifts to the living.[2] They are signposts. Where I live in Sydney there are big red warning signs at motorway exits. They let you know when you're at risk of driving into oncoming traffic. The signs say *wrong way*!

According to the dying, we're going the wrong way when we spend our lives prioritising meeting the expectations of others over boldly showing up as our real selves.

We might see this in daily life as:

- staying in unrewarding relationships

- staying in unrewarding work

- waiting for good things to happen rather than making them happen

- not asking for what we want

- not establishing boundaries – around our time, energy and space

- hiding rather than stepping up and being seen

- complying with society's expectations for how 'people like us' ought to behave

- keeping quiet instead of speaking up

- living smaller, safer, more timid lives.

---

2   The others, in order, are: 'I wish I hadn't worked so hard'; 'I wish I'd had the courage to express my feelings'; 'I wish I'd stayed in touch with my friends'; 'I wish that I had let myself be happier'.

Swipe Right on Your Best Self is a book about boldly choosing to show up as our best selves more often. It's about the practical steps we can take to avoid going the wrong way.

THE COURAGE MYTH

You've already made courageous choices many times in your life. You've used many different strategies to do what was important but challenging. Perhaps you've used sheer willpower, gritty determination, being fiercely self-disciplined or just getting on with it. Sometimes, one or more of these approaches will work.

But not always.

My father served in the Royal Air Force during the Second World War. He was a Hurricane fighter pilot. He died when I was five, so although I never really knew him personally, I grew up with his legend. The mythical version of my father was an amalgam of the pilots I'd seen in Second World War films such as *The Battle of Britain* and *The Dam Busters*. These courageous men ran to their planes at dawn, struggling into flying jackets before taking off to boldly fight the German Luftwaffe. I watched bomber aircrews dodge flak to heroically fly low to blow up dams above German arms factories. I conjured up a fantasy of RAF pilots as fearless aviators on heroic missions.

As an adult, I learnt that the truth was more nuanced. Certainly there *was* incredible courage, but there was also fear, horror, dread, terror and guilt. Fighting for your life each day, in the air or on the ground, is psychologically exhausting. Inevitably, many pilots suffered from debilitating stress, flashbacks and nightmares. Today this condition would be diagnosed as post-traumatic stress disorder (PTSD), a normal human response to traumatic circumstances. However, PTSD wasn't understood back then. Pilots unable to fly were urged to 'get a grip' or 'use more willpower'. If it worked at all, it only worked briefly. Those unable to return to duty were given the shameful diagnosis of 'LMF': low moral fibre. It was assumed their problem wasn't a result of the horrific predicament they found themselves in. No, they had been revealed as deficient human beings. Inherently flawed. My father didn't receive this cruel diagnosis, but he saw many of his fellow pilots condemned in this way.

We're somewhat wiser now, but it's still sometimes assumed that when we don't do what's difficult we're lacking some right stuff. We are deficient. Our culture might diagnose us as lacking courage or willpower. You might even diagnose yourself this way, treating yourself generously with the most impotent of cures: self-criticism. What's often overlooked is the situation. The predicament in which we find ourselves.

I've learned from thought leaders in modern behavioural science that everyday courage isn't some mysterious inner stuff. Taking courageous action is an ability, a skill to develop. Our capacity to use this skill is powerfully influenced by our predicaments. And the quality of our lives depends in large part on how well we can manage our predicaments, develop the skill of taking courageous action and use it to lead lives true to ourselves.

The ideas in this book include the most effective and emotionally intelligent approaches to living courageously I've learned across two Masters degrees in human behaviour change and in over 10 years working as a leadership development specialist in Australia, China and Papua New Guinea. These have been harvested from behavioural, cognitive and neuroscience fields to help you courageously live, love and lead. They are simple approaches that help us define our own missions and skilfully pilot our minds to effectively meet life's challenges.

In *Swipe Right on Your Best Self*, I'll show you how having the courage to live a life true to yourself is eroded by three human predicaments. If we neglect these, we'll continue to waste effort using ineffectual strategies and wonder gloomily what's wrong with us.

We'll begin by understanding what the predicaments are and how they hold us back. Then we'll look at three ways we can get fit for purposeful living – three mental stances to embolden your mind – and conclude with three simple strategies for taking bold action daily. In the final chapter I present a simple seven-step model for swiping right on your best self. These seven steps will help you put courage over comfort for the adventure of a lifetime. Yours.

There are two things I've enjoyed about some books I've read recently. Firstly, I like the ones that get to the point and don't waste my time with excessive padding. This is such a book. Secondly, I appreciate having any references at the end of the chapter, not only at the back of the book. (Don't make me go there!) So I've put my references to sources and further reading, along with links to videos and apps, at the end of each chapter. You're welcome.

As you read this book I encourage you to discard all ideas that don't resonate with you, and embrace those that do. Just one idea may make all the difference. *You* are best placed to discover how you can swipe right on your best self more often, at work and at home. *You* get to choose.

The world we're living in needs more people to take daily courageous action. To say *no* to redundant and toxic ways of treating ourselves, each other and our planet. To say *yes* to lives of greater authenticity and fewer regrets.

READING AND VIEWING

- Frankl, Victor. *Man's Search for Meaning*. Beacon Press, 2006.

- Perel, Esther. *The State of Affairs: Rethinking infidelity*. HarperCollins, 2018.

- School of Life. *Confidence*. www.youtube.com/watch?v=1D-vyjQIUDc.

- Ware, Bronnie. *The Top Five Regrets of the Dying: A life transformed by the dearly departing*. Hay House, 2019.

Part I

HUMAN PREDICAMENTS

'If I were given one hour to save the planet,
I would spend 55 minutes defining the problem
and five minutes resolving it.'

ANONYMOUS

The most important step in creating an effective solution is accurately defining the problem.

Throughout history, people have come up with some pretty weird ideas for what causes distress and disease. It defies belief, but from ancient Greece right up until the 17th century it was thought that an array of women's complaints such as fatigue, vertigo, breathing difficulties and mental anguish were caused by – wait for it – a 'wandering womb'. The womb was thought to be like an animal which could move about the body if unhappy. And what upsets wombs? Why, bad smells and not having enough children. Women unhelpfully diagnosed with this fantasy condition were labelled as hysterical. Wombs were encouraged to return to their proper position with sweet fragrances and then kept in place by having plenty of children.

In this part we'll take a look at three human predicaments that, if left unchecked, will keep each of us living smaller, more fearful and timid lives. How we actually go about addressing these predicaments will be covered throughout the rest of this book. But first, we need to understand what makes having the courage to live a life true to ourselves so challenging.

Chapter 1

WE LIVE IN
TWO WORLDS

'It's difficult to make predictions,
especially about the future.'

DANISH PROVERB

Life on Earth arose about 3.5 billion years ago. The first single-celled organisms, much like today's amoebas, are thought to have been motivated by just two things: moving towards what's wanted, and away from what's not wanted. Towards warmth and away from cold. Towards light and away from dark. Towards rewards and away from what's unpleasant.

MOVE AWAY FROM   **MOVE TOWARDS**

↑   ↓

WHAT'S NOT WANTED   **WHAT'S WANTED**

I used to think that more complex life evolved right away. Quite the opposite. Single-celled aquatic life was the only game in town for another 2.9 billion years. Finally, as recently as 600 million years ago, multi-cellular life evolved, and things began to get bigger. Much bigger. The largest animal on Earth is the mighty blue whale at over 30 metres long and weighing in at a hefty 150,000 kilograms. That's about the same length as the original Boeing 737, and almost four times as heavy. It's bigger than any dinosaur, and is still with us today despite almost being hunted to extinction early in the 20th century.

Despite their size and complexity, blue whales have the same motivation strategy as their one-celled ancestors. They move towards what they want more of, say huge swarms of tasty krill, and away from what's not wanted, say killer whales or whaling ships.

THERE BE DRAGONS

Many incredible creatures have emerged over the last 600 million years, all of them following the same motivation blueprint. Did you know there were once dragons? Not fire-breathing ones perhaps, but massive soaring predators nonetheless. The fantastic quetzalcoatlus was a carnivorous pterosaur flying over North America about 100 million years ago. It had an 11-metre wingspan. That's just one metre less than the Hurricane fighter plane my father flew.

DRAGON HAWKER HURRICANE

Humans weren't around when those flying monsters were swooping down for dinner. Good thing too. I'd never have left my cave. The pterosaurs and dinosaurs mostly died out 66 million years ago, and we have only been around for 300,000 years.

People have been anxious for a long time, however, about imaginary dragons. They appear in legends and fables, originally as terrible sea creatures. A copper globe made in 1510 actually has the words 'here be dragons' written just off the south-east coast of Asia.[1] Humans have an

---

1   It's actually written in Latin: 'Hic sunt dracones'. This appears on one of the first European globes ever made, known as the Hunt-Lenox Globe, which is in the possession of the New York Public Library.

exceptional talent for dreaming up terrible threats, and then navigating away from them.

OUR OWN VIRTUAL REALITY

While all animals inhabit the outer world, humans also occupy an inner world. A world of thoughts, beliefs, memories, predictions, plans, expectations, feelings and daydreams. One Harvard University study[2] estimated we spend 47% of our waking lives 'in our heads'. No other animal has such a sophisticated ability to remember, rehearse and be influenced by things that do not exist in the real world. We are motivated by ideas. It's a terrific skill – which comes at a high price.

If you were to design a virtual reality to spend half your life in, surely you would choose to make it a happy place to be? A world of joy, love, achievement and fun? But mostly we don't. Our attention often slips into an inner world in which we relive past mistakes, hurts and disappointments. Alternatively, we fret over fearful futures, anxiously

2   'A Wandering Mind is an Unhappy Mind', Matthew A. Killingsworth and Daniel Gilbert. *Science*. 12 Nov 2010. Vol. 330, Issue 6006, pp. 932

exploring the many ways things might turn out horribly wrong. Again and again.

Why spend so much time imagining terrible things instead of terrific ones? Well, our ancestors were not at the top of the food chain. They were in it. They were food. What kind of food? Slow, individually vulnerable and nutritious. Certain mindsets keep you alive for longer when you're on the menu. Vigilant and cautious. Pragmatic pessimism pays when you're prey.

This is charmingly demonstrated by the African meerkat, standing on hind legs, watchful for real threats on the horizon or in the sky. We're pretty much the same, scanning our world for risks – but we're seldom so cute. We inherited a cautious genetic legacy that kept our ancestors alive long enough to have equally anxious descendents.

Because it was more important to avoid becoming dinner than it was to find dinner, we developed a negativity bias – the urge to avoid threats is stronger than the urge to approach rewards. When real threats do arise, just like animals, we experience an automatic fight-or-flight response. Action stations! Muscles tense, blood pressure surges, cortisol releases energy. This enables a life-saving dash for safety, or if absolutely necessary, a fight for life. But once the real threat has passed, animals do something very different to us. They settle down and get on with living in the real world around them right now. They live in the present.

Not us. We don't only scan the landscape for threats; we also scan our inner worlds. And we quickly find what we're looking for. There are dangers in our memories, in anxious interpretations of the present and in fearful futures. We too experience a fight-or-flight response, our physiology in a state of alarmed arousal, ready to defend our very lives. Against something that isn't really there.

It's exhausting living defensively.

WHAT IF?

Of course, we also imagine wonderful things – new relationships, getting fitter or leaner, pursuing our personal passions, making good stuff happen. And we feel the urge to move towards what we want more of. Milliseconds later our minds scan for possible threats that might arise on the way.

What if?

What if I'm rejected, what if I fail, what if others disapprove, what if there are dragons? Fearful inner voices predict permanent, irrecoverable suffering and counsel backing off for now.

Trying harder to force ourselves to do what our minds believe is dangerous only serves to amplify fears. Willpower will work occasionally, but often it's an extremely emotionally unintelligent approach and disrespectful of the complexity of the human mind.

The urge to avoid threats is stronger than the urge to approach rewards. Our risk-averse autopilot is easily activated and we can find ourselves taking immediate action to move away from distress.

We procrastinate.

We abandon our hopes.

We soothe ourselves with food, drink, drugs or distractions.

We make excuses.

We blame.

The result is an almost immediate sense of relief. Ahh, that feels *much* better. However, short-term relief comes at the high cost of long-term disappointment – and the number one regret of the dying.

Understanding this human predicament allows us to take the steps necessary to intelligently manage it:

- We can manage our relationship with our inner world, dialling up the appeal of doing what matters, and dialling down the influence of fears and self-doubts.

- We can skilfully pilot the human mind in a way that reduces reactive, defensive and avoidant behaviours, and increases proactive, intentional and courageous actions.

- We can be a little less self-critical when we notice anxiety arising. It's human.

READING

- Hanson, Rick. *Confronting the Negativity Bias.* www.rickhanson.net/ how-your-brain-makes-you-easily-intimidated/.

- Meyer, Robinson. *No Old Maps Actually Say 'Here be Dragons'. But an Ancient Globe Does.* www.theatlantic.com/technology/ archive/2013/12/o-old-maps-actually-say-here-be-dragons/282267/.

CHAPTER SUMMARY

- All animals are motivated to approach rewards and avoid threats in the physical world.

- The urge to avoid threats is stronger than the urge to approach rewards.

- Humans also live in an inner world of thoughts, feelings, memories and imagination.

- The urge to avoid experiencing threats in the inner world nudges us away from living boldly authentic lives in the outer world.

- Understanding human motivation helps us to develop emotionally intelligent ways to reduce natural reactivity, defensiveness and avoidance.

Chapter 2

OUR MODERN JUNK VALUES

'There is almost nothing outside of you that will help
in any kind of lasting way unless you're waiting for
an organ. You can't buy, achieve or date serenity and
peace of mind. This is the most horrible truth and
I so resent it. But it's an inside job.'

ANNE LAMOTT

In the film version of J.R.R. Tolkein's *The Lord of the Rings: The Two Towers*, we see the great wooden hall of Rohan perched atop a rocky hill surrounded by vast empty plains. Our company of heroes step inside, past heavy doors richly decorated with carvings painted in gold. The hall is dark, the lofty roof supported by massive wooden pillars. A few beams of sunlight from high windows penetrate the gloom. At the head of the long hall, sunlight illuminates a three-step dais with an ornate wooden throne. Behind the throne hang coloured banners of cloth with images of white horses, the symbols of the once-proud Kingdom of Rohan.

King Théoden sits on his throne, crowned but slumped, his eyes glassy and faded. He has the authority to lead, but is powerless to exercise it. The reason sits on a bench to his left. Gríma Wormtongue, the pale-faced, black-cloaked counsellor, leans over to whisper another disempowering idea into the king's ear. The king is in a trance and under a spell, obedient to his mischievous counsellor's suggestions. He accepts whatever his odious advisor tells him. In so doing he abdicates his kingly duties. The Kingdom of Rohan is leaderless, and vulnerable to an approaching hostile army.

Luckily for Théoden, Gandalf the White Wizard wields his magical staff to shatter the trance and awaken the king. Théoden suddenly realises just how poisonous Wormtongue's messages have been. He throws him out of the hall and banishes him from his land. His power to choose for himself is restored, and he courageously takes charge of his kingdom once more. He has reclaimed his authority to lead himself and his people.

THE INNER COUNSELLOR

We are all vulnerable to whispers that entrance, eroding our ability to choose for ourselves. From the moment we are born, we are immersed in a world of messages. Messages from culture, organisations and families that tell us explicitly or subtly what's important in life (from *their* perspective). What is expected. How someone like you ought to look, live and love. What others will accept as evidence of success. Once the rules for winning the game of life have been absorbed, our own inner counsellor whispers them back to us. While the trance is intact, we do as we're told. We live the life others expect of us. Sometimes this will align with our own interests. But not always. At times it will not be true to ourselves. We are not living with authenticity.

WE ARE WHAT WE EAT

Our contemporary western culture drip feeds us a variety of messages about living well. Culturally endorsed aspirations for a good life are generously fed to us through film, TV, advertising, social media, in shopping malls and in the news.

Some of it is nourishing – but much amounts to a steady diet of junk values and unhealthy ideas. These messages are designed to exploit the first human predicament: they take advantage of our ability to imagine threats that do not exist – they debilitate us for their own advantage.

Here are my top six toxic myths we're fed by our culture – these are especially visible through advertising, which needs you to feel dissatisfied to drive consumption.

TOXIC MYTH	NOURISHING TRUTH
Happiness is the natural state for all human beings. If you're not happy, something's wrong.[1]	**Happiness is just one of our natural states.** A full life must also include sadness, disappointment, despair, regret, embarrassment and guilt. And much more.
Prioritise pleasure and avoid discomfort for wellbeing. The most important thing is feeling good. Now. You deserve it. Feelings are the best guide to action. When making a decision, ask yourself what you feel like doing. Then do that.	**Instant gratification is a poor strategy for a great life.** People with a high quality of life ask what's personally important. And do that. They feel good later. Life's most worthwhile experiences include a down payment of discomfort – uncertainty, vulnerability, fear and effort, for starters.
You are not enough. You are in fact deficient. Others are more happy, attractive, wealthy, successful, clever, popular, funny, cultured, intelligent or educated. Compare yourself frequently to others to see the truth of your shortcomings. In particular, everyone else is happier than you. You can tell this by comparing how you feel inside to how they look outside. Be more of everything. Compete relentlessly.	**You are inherently worthy.** There will always be others who are more this, that and the other. And that's okay. The characteristics of others neither diminish nor boost your worthiness. Annoyingly exuberant (but phenomenally successful) comedian Jim Carrey says, 'I wish everyone could be rich and famous so they realise that it's not the answer'. Social comparison is an excellent strategy if you need to feel awful. Accept your self-worth *and* develop personal qualities important to you. Enjoy progress.

---

1   See Russ Harris's *The Happiness Trap* for an excellent discussion of cultural myths regarding positivity and effective strategies for managing challenging thoughts and feelings – another five-star book.

TOXIC MYTH	NOURISHING TRUTH
You do not have enough. You need more. Compare what you have to what others have. Do this frequently to see the truth of this. You are what you possess and frankly it's insufficient. Get more of everything.	**You are not your possessions.** Stuff outside of you will not make your insides happy, not for long at any rate. The rich and famous can be deeply depressed and the poor and unknown can enjoy profound wellbeing. Go ahead and enjoy stuff (I do), but it's not a path to enduring wellbeing.
Enoughness can be achieved through consumption. We sell it here. If you're not completely satisfied, you didn't buy enough. Please try harder.	**This game is rigged – play at your peril.** You are already worthy. The promise of pleasure through consumption is never met for long. Learn to want what you already have.
Happiness comes from impressing others. Others will be impressed when you are perfectly enough in all respects. Happiness is an outside job.	**Wellbeing has many sources.** It's futile to tether your wellbeing to the fickle approval of others. Wellbeing is an inside job.

Toxic myths have been whispered to us our entire lives. Johann Hari, journalist and author of *Lost Connections*, believes today's epidemic of depression and anxiety is fuelled by the junk values we're fed. Hari writes:

> *You aren't a machine with broken parts. You are an animal whose needs are not being met. You need to have a community. You need to have meaningful values, not the junk values you've been pumped full of all your life, telling you happiness comes through money and buying objects. You need to have meaningful work. You need the natural world. You need to feel you are respected. You need a secure future.*

TOXIC POSITIVITY

The original German folk stories collected in the 19th century by the Brothers Grimm were pretty bleak. Occasional happy endings were eclipsed by drownings, murders, cannibalism, blindings, slavery and sexual assault. Since then, these gruesome tales have had repeated positivity makeovers. Now everyone lives happily ever after. Except for the bad guys. They always get punished. In fairy tales.

Little Red Riding Hood's persistent positivity takes a nose dive

Our Western culture appears to have experienced a thorough positivity makeover too. We are relentlessly encouraged to think exclusively positively, looking only on the bright side, regardless of our immediate circumstances:

- 'Lost a job? Good for you; you're free to get a better one.'

- 'Dumped? Plenty more fish in the sea!'

- 'Death of a close one? They're in a better place.'

Having or voicing painful experiences is increasingly prohibited. Swift reassurances may be well meaning, but skating over distress invalidates the legitimate suffering essential to recovery. We do this to others, and we do this to ourselves. It's inauthentic to deny difficulties and, importantly, it depletes courage.

The ability to take a positive perspective *is* a useful skill to develop, especially with a human mind that comes pre-skilled with an uncanny ability to notice what's wrong. However, more is not always better. When we overdose on positivity at the expense of acknowledging our challenging experiences we do ourselves and others an enormous disservice. Courageous living demands an emotional agility – the ability to acknowledge negative experiences *and* do what's worthwhile.

An honest stance is a courageous one.

IT'S A WONDERFUL LIFE, EXCEPT WHEN IT ISN'T

Children called to bed have been known to stick fingers in their ears and cry out 'can't hear you!' Adults are also expert at refusing to accept unpalatable truths regarding our human circumstances. David Benatar, head of the Department of Philosophy at the University of Cape Town, writes bluntly on the matter. His boldly pessimistic premise is that life is much harder than we dare acknowledge. I think he's right. Here are some of his reasons laid out in his bleakly funny, and yet curiously reassuring, book *The Human Predicament*:

- People want to feel younger but age relentlessly into weakness and decrepitude.

- There's chronic pain but no chronic pleasure – any happiness is fleeting.

- We get sick and hurt quickly but heal slowly.

- Most of our life's desires will remain unfulfilled.

- Desires which are fulfilled satisfy less than expected; jobs are less interesting and spouses more irritating.

- We can't get no satisfaction but strive with futility to achieve it.

- Life is brief. There is more bad than good in it. Then you die.

- King or pauper, you will be quickly forgotten and all traces of your life will vanish.

- There is no cosmic meaning. Your life is pointless from a planetary perspective.

After reading this gloomy assessment you might imagine he would be advocating immediate self-destruction to avoid certain misery and save time. Far from it. He states:

The absence of any – even terrestrial – meaning is best addressed not by taking one's own life, but by attempting to invest one's life with some meaning.

The implausibly multi-talented comedian Tim Minchin also advocated taking responsibility for making life meaningful in his 2013 commencement speech at the University of Western Australia:

I said at the beginning of this ramble that life is meaningless. It was not a flippant assertion. I think it's absurd: the idea of seeking 'meaning' in the set of circumstances that happens to exist after 13.8 billion years' worth of unguided events. Leave it to humans to think the universe has a purpose for them. However, I am no nihilist. I am not even a cynic. I am, actually, rather romantic. And here's my idea of romance:

you will soon be dead. Life will sometimes seem long and tough and, god, it's tiring. And you will sometimes be happy and sometimes sad. And then you'll be old. And then you'll be dead. There is only one sensible thing to do with this empty existence, and that is: fill it. Not fillet. Fill. It. And in my opinion (until I change it), life is best filled by learning as much as you can about as much as you can, taking pride in whatever you're doing, having compassion, sharing ideas, running, being enthusiastic. And then there's love, and travel, and wine, and sex, and art, and kids, and giving, and mountain climbing ... but you know all that stuff already. It's an incredibly exciting thing, this one, meaningless life of yours.

Benatar suggests adopting a stance of pragmatic pessimism, in which we courageously accept our predicament but do not allow it to overwhelm us, instead doing all we can to enhance the quality of life for ourselves, other humans and other animals. From Benatar's perspective, this realistic, honest and proactive stance 'makes one's life less bad than it would be if one allowed the predicament to overwhelm one to the point where one was perpetually gloomy and dysfunctional, although it is also compatible with moments or periods of despair, protest, or rage about being forced to accept the unacceptable'.

Although we might consciously reject those toxic myths regarding happiness, an unconscious (or subconscious or nonconscious) part of us is paying careful attention. I'll use the term 'unconscious' throughout this book to refer to that part of us of which we are largely unaware. Our unconscious beliefs have much more influence on what we say and do when we're tired, stressed or distracted. That's when we enter our own reactive waking trance. When we're most susceptible to the whispers of our inner counsellor. As you will have doubtless noticed, the modern world excels at keeping us tired, stressed *and* distracted.

To some degree, the junk values we've been fed quietly discourage all of us, sapping our capacity to lean boldly into life. When we abdicate the leadership of our own lives, we trade away our power to:

- set our own bold and exciting directions (instead living smaller, safer, more muted lives)

- choose what matters to us (instead nodding as relentless marketing dictates what matters to others)

- choose our own identities (instead conforming to socially sanctioned roles)

- live with passionate personal purpose (instead surrendering our life energy to obediently build the pyramids of pharaohs by fulfilling the purposes of other organisations, groups or individuals).

As an act of courageous subversive defiance we can recognise and reject the junk values we are fed. Instead we can consciously choose for ourselves what's important, learn to awaken from our reactive trances and live with courageous authenticity.

READING AND VIEWING

- Benatar, David. *The Human Predicament: A candid guide to life's biggest questions.* Oxford University Press, 2017.

- Hari, Johann. *Lost Connections: Why you're depressed and how to find hope.* Bloomsbury Publishing, 2019.

- Harris, Russ. *The Happiness Trap: How to stop struggling and start living: a guide to ACT.* Trumpeter, 2008.

- *The Lord of the Rings: The Two Towers.* Directed by Peter Jackson. 2002.

- Lamott, Anne. *TED: 12 Truths I Learned from Life and Writing.* 2017. www.ted.com/talks/anne_lamott_12_truths_i_learned_ from_life_and_writing.

- Minchin, Tim. *Occasional Address.* 25 September 2013. www.timminchin.com/2013/09/25/occasional-address/.

- Morfin, Marcelina. *13 Twisted Fairy Tales by the Brothers Grimm.* www.theculturetrip.com/europe/germany/articles/13-intriguing-fairy-tales-by-the-brothers-grimm/.

CHAPTER SUMMARY

- Society tells us repeatedly that happiness is normal and that the unhappy are abnormal.

- Advertising says you are insufficient, but you can fill the gap with purchases and achieve happiness through impressing others.

- Junk values weaken us and sap courageous living.

- The cultural emphasis on positivity prohibits making space for painful feelings.

- A life fully lived must include the full gamut of emotions, the pleasant and unpleasant.

- A courageous life is achieved by choosing your own values, and waking up every day and filling your life with meaning, even when it's challenging. Which it will be. Often.

Chapter 3

THE BIGGEST ELEPHANT

'I intend to live forever. So far, so good.'

STEVEN WRIGHT

If life on Earth is a vast ocean, then individual lives are the waves. Waves that arise, travel some distance and break upon a shore. How long does a wave last? Life spans for animals range from just 14 days for a fruit fly to over 500 chilly years for Icelandic clams. The longest living person to date has been Jeanne Louise Calment, a French woman who lived until she was 122. You might well be wondering how Madame Calment achieved her world record. Did she take vitamins, cold showers, was she vegetarian? She did indeed follow a strict regime in later life. Ready? Here's what she did (mind that this may or may not work for you). She started each day being grateful for what she had, ate dessert after every meal and finished each day with a Dunhill cigarette and a glass of port.

Vive la France!

Fruit fly, clam or person, individual lives on Earth are preceded by almost 14 billion years of not being. Then a flash of life. Followed by an unfathomably longer period of not being. All living things die. But humans appear to be in a unique predicament.

We know.

LOOKING BEYOND THE PRESENT

According to Martin Seligman, a leading authority in the field of positive psychology and Director of the University of Pennsylvania Positive Psychology Center, human success as a species rests on one ability: anticipation. Our unique capacity to look beyond the present and imagine what might lay ahead.

As far as we can tell, animals don't ponder what tomorrow might bring. They don't worry about the future. They don't consciously plan ahead. Their attention is in the present moment, experiencing whatever is actually happening now. Squirrels may appear to intentionally bury nuts with an eye to next year but the action is entirely instinctual. It would be mean, but you can activate this ancient instinct in caged squirrels indoors by giving them some nuts and then reducing the daylight hours with artificial lighting to simulate the approach of winter. Enthusiastic nut burying quickly ensues, but only if you shorten daylight hours.

As discussed earlier, humans live in an outer world *and* an inner world. Reliving the past. Evaluating the present. Pre-living possible futures. Our negativity bias drives the diligent rehearsal of potential future problems and the exploration of possible solutions. Especially at 3 am!

At some point in our past, an early human ancestor would have noticed that animals were born and then they died. They also noticed that other people followed a similar path. They then did a little imaginative time travel and came to a disturbing conclusion. They too would die one day.

Our imaginations may set us apart from other animal life but we do share a biological imperative. Stay alive. Do not get killed. This prime directive trumps all other urges. First avoid death, *then* go ahead and hunt, eat, have sex, make art – but above all, stay alive. As the Bee Gees put it, 'whether you're a brother or whether you're a mother, you're stayin' alive, stayin' alive'. This Bee Gees instinct has been part of the mammalian blueprint for over 300 million years.

So what happens when you combine the ancient biological imperative that *you must not die* with the human awareness that *you must die*? Behold! The third human predicament. The tension between these two ideas can be unbearable. Personal annihilation is unacceptable *and also unavoidable*. All other animal life is spared this appalling insight. And our predicament is, incredibly, slightly worse than at first sight. Not only will you certainly die eventually, but you might die much, much sooner, say through accident or illness. One way or another, death is imminent.

At this point another biological urge generally kicks in. Move away from the threatening idea. Use that problem-solving brain to make the distress go away. Quick!

Humans are of course quite expert at not engaging with distressing realities. Each of us is talented at ignoring uncomfortable truths. We are self-delusion specialists. Moreover, we happily collude with one another in not mentioning what must be the biggest elephant in the room of life.

Popular self-soothing strategies offering instant relief include:

- *Avoidance.* It may be true but what's the point in dwelling on it?

- *Distraction.* Put your attention anywhere else. Work, sex, food, Netflix, Facebook, the news, Twitter, Instagram. Keep that phone charged. Buy that new TV. So much choice!

- *Numbing.* Mute your distress with alcohol or other mind-altering substances. More affordable and accessible than ever.

- *Denial.* We don't really die. We persist in some mysterious way.

Maybe there is life after death. I don't think so, but how could anyone know? ('Because it's in print,' doesn't strike me as compelling evidence.) As far as *this* book is concerned, it doesn't matter if we endure beyond death or not. This is a book about courageously living a life true to yourself while you have an earthly pulse.

> 'Live not as though there were a thousand years
> ahead of you. Fate is at your elbow; make yourself
> good while life and power are still yours.'
>
> **MARCUS AURELIUS**

The real question is, what are the consequences of rejecting or accepting our predicament?

REJECTION: UPSIDES	REJECTION: DOWNSIDES
• Feels good now!	• Energy is required to keep a threatening idea out of mind. It can be gently draining, leaving you depleted, reactive and defensive.
	• Like an outstanding tax return, awareness will occasionally creep back to haunt you – total avoidance is impossible.
	• Your time alive is your most precious resource. It's irreplaceable. When we push the brevity of our lives out of mind we devalue our time and risk squandering it.
	• We sap ourselves of any urgency to do what matters now. There's always tomorrow! We procrastinate our very lives away.

ACCEPTANCE: UPSIDES	ACCEPTANCE: DOWNSIDES
• Ignites an urgency to take courageous action now, while we can.	• Wistful regret.
• Time is spent meaningfully – you're not prepared to exchange it for frivolous things.	
• Magnifies an appreciation, gratitude and valuing of our days.	
• More energy available for engaging with life and loved ones.	

We need an emotionally intelligent way to effectively handle this pessimistic predicament. An honest way that will boost vitality and dissolve despair.

READING AND VIEWING

- Bee Gees. *Stayin' Alive* (Official Music Video). www.youtube.com/watch?v=fNFzfwLM72c.

- The School of Life. *I Am Going to Die!* www.youtube.com/watch?v=Mn4AE44npek.

- Seligman, Martin, Peter Railton, Roy F. Baumeister and Chandra Sripada. *Homo Prospectus*. Oxford University Press, 2016.

CHAPTER SUMMARY

- Humans alone are aware of their mortality.

- The reluctance to accept the unacceptable triggers defence strategies to keep the fact out of conscious awareness.

- The price of self-delusion is a devaluing of life and a sapping of urgency for courageous living.

Part II

FIT FOR PURPOSE

'We choose to go to the Moon in this decade and do the other things, not because they are easy, but because they are hard; because that goal will serve to organize and measure the best of our energies and skills, because that challenge is one that we are willing to accept, one we are unwilling to postpone, and therefore as we set sail we ask God's blessing on the most hazardous and dangerous and greatest adventure on which man has ever embarked.'

US PRESIDENT JOHN F. KENNEDY, 1961

The United States was deeply embarrassed. The space race was conspicuously being lost to Cold War rival the Soviet Union. Sputnik, the world's first artificial satellite, had been launched by the Soviets in 1957. Only 58 centimetres in diameter, it represented a huge technological breakthrough. The world looked on, astonished. Then in April 1961 Russian cosmonaut Yuri Gagarin became the first man in space. Newspapers across the US reported this as an American failure, not a Soviet success. The Americans' sense of superiority had been badly dented. Weren't capitalism and technological superiority supposed to be inextricably linked? Something had to be done. Something big. And quickly.

Just six weeks later, on 25 May 1961, President Kennedy made his jaw-dropping announcement: 'I believe that this nation should commit itself to achieving the goal, before this decade is out, of landing a man on the Moon and returning him safely to the Earth.'

The goal was staggeringly bold and ambitious. The Apollo Program team didn't know how they could do it. But they knew why. To move away from shame and towards pride. To restore the identity of the United States as the pre-eminently superior global culture through achieving what would be mankind's greatest achievement.

The pressure was on. Pressure that would inspire courage and success. Pressure that would cause mistakes and failure.

The initial task for NASA was to develop a strategy. The most intuitive approach was to build a gargantuan rocket to fly directly to the Moon, land there and fly back. Straight there, straight back, one vehicle.

This simple strategy had considerable support and was set to receive endorsement. But John Houbolt, a middle-ranking NASA engineer, thought this was preposterous. He saw it as a clumsy and needlessly costly brute-force approach to the challenge. Instead, he advocated a non-intuitive but elegantly agile solution known as the Lunar Orbit Rendezvous. This would involve sending a much smaller vehicle from Earth to orbit around the moon. A lunar lander would then separate, head to the moon's surface, and return to reconnect with the orbiter (both moving through space as they did so!) before returning to Earth. John courageously challenged the consensus of his colleagues, and broke with protocol and addressed his concerns directly to senior NASA administration. Who initially scoffed. And then were persuaded.

The next years were a frenzy of activity. Under intense time constraints, corners were cut, safety was neglected and production was rushed. Courageous voices willing to challenge authority were quiet in the headlong rush to get it done. The inside of the capsule was lined with combustible materials such as Velcro and nylon. The atmosphere in the capsule was 100% oxygen under pressure. The capsule hatch had been designed to open inwards, and there was no way of getting out in less than a minute and a half in the event of an emergency. The wiring was sloppy. The build had been rushed. The craft simply wasn't fit for purpose. But on they pushed.

In February 1967, Gus Grissom, Edward White and Roger Chaffee crawled into the command module to test the launch procedure. The spacecraft was unfuelled; they were merely testing the procedure and equipment for a later launch. They sat suited up in cramped conditions for four hours as test after test failed. Then disaster struck. Fire. A spark from exposed wiring ignited a furious burning of multiple combustible materials within the capsule, accelerated by oxygen at high pressure. There was no time to get out. Intense temperatures rapidly melted the crews' face masks and they quickly succumbed to smoke and carbon monoxide poisoning. It took five minutes before workers could open the hatch from the outside.

It was far too late.

EXTREME OWNERSHIP

Three days later, Gene Kranz, NASA Flight Director for the Apollo program, called the branch and flight control team together and made the following announcement:

Spaceflight will never tolerate carelessness, incapacity, and neglect. Somewhere, somehow, we screwed up. It could have been in design, build, or test. Whatever it was, we should have caught it. We were too gung ho about the schedule and we locked out all of the problems we saw each day in our work.

Every element of the program was in trouble and so were we. The simulators were not working, Mission Control was behind in virtually every area, and the flight and test procedures changed daily. Nothing we did had any shelf life. Not one of us stood up and said, 'Dammit, stop!' I don't know what Thompson's committee will find as the cause, but I know what I find. We are the cause! We were not ready! We did not do our job. We were rolling the dice, hoping that things would come together by launch day, when in our hearts we knew it would take a miracle. We were pushing the schedule and betting that the Cape would slip before we did.

From this day forward, Flight Control will be known by two words: 'Tough' and 'Competent.' Tough means we are forever accountable for what we do or what we fail to do. We will never again compromise our responsibilities. Every time we walk into Mission Control we will know what we stand for. Competent means we will never take anything for granted. We will never be found short in our knowledge and in our skills. Mission Control will be perfect.

When you leave this meeting today you will go to your office and the first thing you will do there is to write 'Tough and Competent' on your blackboards. It will never be erased. Each day when you enter the room these words will remind you of the price paid by Grissom, White, and Chaffee. These words are the price of admission to the ranks of Mission Control.

The lessons learnt from what became known as the Apollo 1 disaster transformed the Apollo space mission. The new culture of enhanced accountability, ownership and courage to speak up made the ultimate Apollo 11 moon landing on 20 July 1969 possible.

OUR GREATEST ADVENTURE

To live a life true to ourselves is the greatest adventure we shall undertake. It requires courageously choosing our own rewarding directions, not because they are easy, but because they are hard. It demands navigating through challenges that we are willing to accept, and unwilling to postpone. A courageous life requires a craft fit for purpose.

Our minds and bodies are the vehicles we use to navigate life. When we neglect them, we set ourselves up for disappointment, inevitably becoming more reactive, defensive and avoidant – more likely to lead the lives others expect of us. When we take care of our craft, we become increasingly proactive, intentional and courageous. Better able to live lives true to ourselves.

There are three simple ways we can make courageous living much easier. These are things you're already doing every day. Small adjustments now can lead to significant changes in your authentic trajectory through life. How you *sleep, move* and *eat* determine to what extent you're fit for purpose. They're each important, but one is even more critical than the other two, so we'll start there.

Chapter 4

SLEEPING TIGHTLY NIGHTLY

'Sleep is not an optional lifestyle luxury.
It is a non-negotiable biological necessity.
It is your life support system.'

MATTHEW WALKER

For millennia, people have gone down with the sun. We've recharged in the dark and risen re-energised at dawn. A short snooze early afternoon provided an extra boost. Hunter-gatherer tribes in Northern Kenya still live this way, sleeping for eight to eight-and-half-hours each day.

We can thank (and blame) Humphry Davy, an English chemist and inventor, for creating the first electric lamp in 1802. People then had another good 77 years of natural sleep before the American inventor Thomas Edison and his team developed the first practical and inexpensive lightbulb in 1879. Today we choose when our suns set. And we often choose late.

Many of us are still getting up early (to beat the traffic) but we also choose to stay up late, working or entertaining ourselves with 24-hour access to Netflix, YouTube, email and Instagram. And if external distractions don't keep us up, internal ones may step in. Busy minds fret over what's left undone and the challenges tomorrow will bring. Charlotte Brontë hit the insomniac's nail on the head when she wrote: 'A ruffled mind makes a restless pillow.'

A 2019 report for the Sleep Health Foundation conducted by the University of South Australia found that 60% of Australians experience sleep difficulties three or more times every week. Globally, about 50% of adults in developed countries don't get the sleep they need.

HOW MUCH SLEEP IS ENOUGH?

Does it really matter if we sleep less, either willingly or unwillingly? How much sleep do we really need anyway?

In his extraordinary book *Why We Sleep*, leading sleep researcher Professor Matthew Walker describes how getting less than seven to nine hours of quality sleep negatively impacts every system in the body.

That's right. *Every* system. Some of us only need seven hours. Some of us nine.

You can operate on less, but there are hidden costs. A lack of sleep over just one night:

- reduces emotional intelligence, making you more reactive and negative

- undermines decision making (we're dumber when we sleep less)

- increases appetite, stopping you from noticing when you're full and boosting fat storage – a triple-whammy burger

- prevents learning by failing to put what you learnt during the day into long-term memory (it's like going to the trouble of writing a document on a computer and not bothering to actually save it)

- demolishes the immune system (routinely sleeping less than six hours a night even doubles the risk of cancer).

Over the longer term, insufficient quality sleep also promotes Alzheimer's disease and dementia. Matthew Walker doesn't pull any punches. He says wakefulness causes low-level brain damage. It's sleep that repairs.

In this book we're concerned about maintaining our minds to help us courageously show up and live a life true to ourselves. How does sleep influence that?

Sleep consists of a number of different phases, such as light sleep, deep sleep and REM (rapid eye movement) sleep. Important things happen in each of them. However, during REM sleep our minds undergo emotional recalibration. This emotional tune-up gives us the resilience necessary to effectively meet tomorrow's tasks, setbacks and challenges. We all know how small children can become emotional when they're tired. Well, the same thing happens to adults. The less you sleep, the more emotionally reactive you become and the less self-control you have. You'll become more tetchy and impulsive, giving into urges. There's a reason shoddy advertising is shown overnight. Those vibrating foot massagers, knife sets and rowing machines are especially appealing to impulsive minds. Don't take a mind like that into work or into a relationship.

REM sleep typically happens five times a night, roughly every 90 minutes. Blocks of REM sleep are longer towards the end of the night. This means that your last hour of sleep is especially rich in REM.

There are two ways many of us cheat ourselves of this critical emotional tune-up. Firstly, we may sleep for less than seven hours, losing that last longer burst of REM. Secondly, we may inadvertently shatter the quality of our REM sleep.

I have some awful news to share on this score. One of the most powerful suppressors of REM sleep is ... alcohol. I'm so sorry. Even low levels of alcohol will interrupt REM to some degree. For optimal REM, avoid alcohol altogether. The more you drink and the closer to going to sleep, the greater the impact.

WHAT TO DO

Most of us neglect our sleep because we just don't realise how important it is. It may have seemed sort of optional. Even a waste of time. Once you realise just how critical sleeping is to your quality of life and your ability to show up as your best, the first step is to give sleep the priority treatment it deserves.

Here are Matthew Walker's top five actionable tips to improve the quality of sleep:

1. Darkness: dim lights in the hour preceding sleep, stay off screens and keep the bedroom as dark as possible while sleeping.

2. Temperature: if possible, set the bedroom temperature to about 18°C/65°F.

3. Don't lie awake in bed for more than 20 minutes.

4. Avoid caffeine after midday.

5. Avoid alcohol.

READING AND VIEWING

- Meadows, Guy. *The Sleep Book: How to Sleep Well Every Night.* Orion, 2015.

- Sleep Health Foundation. *Chronic Insomnia Disorder in Australia.* www.sleephealthfoundation.org.au/news/special-reports/chronic-insomnia-disorder-in-australia.html.

- Walker, Matthew. *Why We Sleep: Unlocking the power of sleep and dreams.* Scribner, 2018.

- Walker, Matthew. 'How to Improve Your Sleep'. www.youtube.com/watch?v=lRp5AC9W_F8&t=185s.

CHAPTER SUMMARY

- To function at your best, you need between seven and nine hours of quality sleep every night.

- Insufficient quality sleep has immediate consequences. Reactivity, negativity and impulsivity go up. Decision making, learning and memory go down.

- The last hour of sleep is disproportionately beneficial for REM sleep and getting the emotional tune-up necessary for courageous living.

- Prioritising sleep is critical to being fit for purpose.

CHAPTER 5

YA LIKE TO MOVE IT MOVE IT

'You have brains in your head. You have feet in your shoes.
You can steer yourself any direction you choose.'

DR SEUSS

There are some very odd things living in the sea. One of them is the humble sea squirt. As a youngster it has a very simple nervous system, just enough to enable it to swim off and look for a home. When it finds a good location it settles down and attaches itself – permanently. It's done roaming. There's commitment for you.

I have some sympathy for this attitude – I've lived in over 20 homes across five countries. I'd say I'm over it too. Relocating is a lot of work. The sea squirt can't be bothered with all that. But what it does next is not something I'm willing to contemplate. As soon as it's chosen a permanent home for life, it eats its own brain. You read that right. It eats and digests its own brain. You see, the purpose of the brain – to move – has been fulfilled. It's just not needed any more. Except as a snack.

In his intriguing TED talk *The Real Reason for Brains*, neuroscientist Daniel Wolpert explains that 'we have a brain for one reason, and one reason only, and that's to produce adaptable and complex movements'. Of course, you can program a robot to perform precise motor movements, such as on an assembly line. But don't ask that same robot to stack a dishwasher, pick an apple or make a bed (don't ask me either). The skills don't transfer. Even children have far greater dexterity. You need a brain for adaptive and complex body movements. You need a brain to navigate. To move.

Just as our muscles improve with use, so does the human brain. Give it a workout and it adapts. It gets better at what it practises. You're probably already familiar with the idea you can train the brain with puzzles, reading and memory challenges – anything that makes you think hard is brain exercise. But you can also build a better brain with movement. Physical activity gives brains a lot of work to do – maintaining balance, moving limbs just the right amount, deciding where and how to place your feet, moving around obstacles. Simply going for a walk is a workout for the brain. Or a cycle. Or a swim. Our brains are intimately linked to our movement. Movement develops our brain because movement requires a brain.

John Ratey, author of *Spark: The revolutionary new science of exercise and the brain*, says:

> ... *more nerve cells fire when we're exercising than when we're doing anything else. This activates the brain as a whole. It turns on arousal, attention, the frontal cortex, the executive functioning area – so we're all set to participate in the world.*

Nerve activity from movement generates brain-derived neurotrophic factor (BDNF), a sort of brain cell fertiliser. Just a little encourages neural growth and new connections. BDNF is created by exercise and spreads throughout the whole brain, promoting development across the brain. This is a bit like lifting weights with one arm and then finding your whole body becoming lean and toned.

Movement also generates neurotransmitters such as norepinephrine, which activates attention, perception and motivation; serotonin, which improves your mood, and lowers impulsivity and irritability; and dopamine, which governs attention and learning, plus our sense of contentment and reward.

Intriguingly, exercise also increases courage and resilience to stress. Active muscles release hormones into the blood stream that researchers have dubbed 'hope molecules'. Our minds and bodies are ever ready to reward movement by making you braver and lifting your spirits. The antidepressant effect of modest amounts of regular exercise has been well researched. However, psychologist Tal Ben-Shahar says that movement is so critical to our wellbeing that *not* exercising is the same as taking a depressant!

'If you are in a bad mood go for a walk.
If you are still in a bad mood go for another walk.'

HIPPOCRATES

Movement activates our happier, smarter and more resilient selves. It makes our minds (and bodies) fit for purposeful living. Movement prepares your mind for courageous choices. Inactivity, on the other hand, makes us all dumber and habitual. That's okay if you're a sea squirt. It's not okay for you.

So what sort of movement will make a difference? All movement counts: standing up, walking, running, swimming, cycling, surfing, table tennis, dancing and so on. More is better, and a variety of movements is optimal. Walking outside in the real world is more stimulating and nourishing than walking on a treadmill. Movement through nature is especially powerful. The Japanese encourage 'shinrin-yoku' or 'forest bathing', the process of making contact with and taking in the atmosphere of the forest. Research shows that spending time in nature lowers cortisol, the pulse rate and blood pressure. It also calms the mind.

Curiously, the mood-boosting benefits of movement are amplified when we do it in the presence of other people. But introverts can relax – it's not necessary to compete in a sports team or take up line dancing if that's not your thing.

The combined benefits of movement, the outdoors and community are exemplified by Parkrun, a global movement which organises free, highly informal, communal five-kilometre runs. The best bit is you don't have to run. You can walk. Bring the dog. Push a pram. If you choose to track your time each week and get stronger and faster, that's entirely up to you. These friendly communal events are a fantastic antidote to our increasingly isolated and inactive modern ways of living. Parkruns are springing up everywhere. Take a look.

It may be tempting to get all your movement done in a single time-efficient block. However, biomechanists like Katy Bowman, author of *Move Your DNA*, recommend moving small amounts throughout the day instead. We've evolved to move. Not sit. Your brain will thank you.

Daniel Pink, author of several provocative bestselling books about business, work, creativity and behaviour, has some simple advice for getting breaks to restore the mind during the day:

- **Something beats nothing.** Don't let your thinking stagnate by working for too long without a break. Research by DeskTime, a productivity tracking software company, found that the most productive people work 52 minutes on and 17 minutes off. Find your own ideal ratio.

- **Moving beats stationary.** Simply standing up and walking around for five minutes each hour is potent. Microbursts of activity like this beat a single block of 30 minutes for improving motivation, concentration and creativity.

- **Social beats solo.** Even introverts like myself can benefit from having a restorative break with others.

- **Outside beats inside.** People underestimate how much more restorative a short walk outdoors is compared to walking indoors.

- **Fully detached beats semi-detached.** If you're having a break, really take a break. Disengage from technology. Notice the outside world. Avoid multi-tasking during your time off.

Another advantage of movement and exercise is the impact on sleep. Matthew Walker, the sleep researcher we met in chapter 4, says 'exercise frequently increases total sleep time, especially deep REM sleep. It also deepens the quality of sleep, resulting in more powerful electrical brainwave activity.' We've already talked about how important sleep is to prepare your mind for courageous choices, like exercising when you don't feel like it. So people who get a good night's sleep are more likely to exercise. And are therefore more likely to sleep well. And are therefore more likely to exercise. And are therefore more likely to sleep well.

You get the idea.

Helen Keller tells us 'life is either a daring adventure, or nothing'. Movement prepares the mind for your daring adventure. Let's get moving.

READING

- Bowman, Katy. *Move Your DNA: Restore your health through natural movement.* Propriometrics Press, 2014.

- McGonigal, Kelly. *The Joy of Movement: How exercise helps us find happiness, hope, connection and courage.* Avery, 2019.

- Pink, Daniel. *When: The scientific secrets of perfect timing.* Riverhead Books, 2018.

- Ratey, John. *Spark: The revolutionary new science of exercise and the brain.* Little, Brown and Company, 2013.

- Wolpert, Daniel. *The Real Reason for Brains.* www.ted.com/talks/daniel_wolpert_the_real_reason_for_brains.

CHAPTER SUMMARY

- Brains evolved for movement.
- Movement develops the brain.
- Movement upgrades your mood and makes you braver.
- Movement makes you fit for purposeful living.
- Move often. Outside if you can. In nature when possible. With others is even better.

Chapter 6

GOOD MOOD FOOD

'One cannot think well, love well, sleep well,
if one has not dined well.'

VIRGINIA WOOLF

The year 2019 marked the 50th anniversary of the Apollo 11 moon flight by Neil Armstrong, Edwin 'Buzz' Aldrin and Michael Collins. To commemorate the event, a documentary film (also named *Apollo 11*) was released showing archive footage of the astronauts, the ground crew and an excited public who turned out to watch. It's a terrific film that really transports you back in time to experience the enormity of the adventure. There are many astonishing scenes in space, but there was one on Earth that grabbed my attention too. It's the morning of 16 July 1969, and the Florida beaches around the Kennedy Space Centre are packed with a public eager to watch history being made. Over 10,000 cars line the roads. The 101-metre Saturn V rocket stands proudly in the summer dawn, illuminated by bright neon lights. People are sitting and standing on cars, walls, any spot they can find, staring into the distance. And there's something odd about most of the people. Something different. They're … slim.

Over the last 50 years, people in many countries have got a lot bigger. And sicker. Rates of obesity, heart disease and diabetes are growing. Diabetes alone is approximately *seven times* more prevalent in the US since the Apollo 11 launch. What can account for this rocketing expansion of waists and ill health? The science of nutrition is in its infancy, and there is considerable disagreement about what constitutes a healthy diet. However, Michael Pollan, author of *In Defense of Food*, cautions against thinking of food in terms of its chemical constituents and points to bigger problems:

> All of our uncertainties about nutrition should not obscure the plain fact that the chronic diseases that now kill most of us can be traced directly to the industrialization of our food: the rise of highly processed foods and refined grains; the use of chemicals to raise plants and animals in huge monocultures; the superabundance of cheap calories of sugar and fat produced by modern agriculture; and the narrowing of the biological diversity of the human diet to

a tiny handful of staple crops, notably wheat, corn, and soy. These changes have given us the Western diet that we take for granted: lots of processed foods and meat, lots of added fat and sugar, lots of everything – except vegetables, fruits, and whole grains.

Where the Western diet is introduced, Western diseases quickly follow. In *Why We Get Fat*, Gary Taubes describes how:

… when isolated populations start eating Western foods, sugar and white flour are inevitably first, because these foods could be transported around the world as items of trade without spoiling or being devoured on the way by rodents and insects. The Inuits, for example, living on seals, caribou, and whale meat, begin eating sugar and flour (crackers and bread). Western diseases follow. The agrarian Kikuyu, living in Kenya, start eating sugar and flour, and these diseases appear. The Maasai add sugar and flour to their diet or move into the cities and begin eating these foods, and the diseases appear.

In this book we're less concerned about how our diet might make us fat or physically sick, and more interested in how what we eat influences our minds and moods. Our ability to think and choose well. Which brings us to your evil twin.

While you are unquestionably admirably balanced, thoughtful and alert, your evil twin who occasionally visits is impulsive, anxious and moody. You are diligent and motivated. Your evil twin prefers to slack off.

THE BLOOD SUGAR ROLLER COASTER

There's one place you're especially likely to find your twin: on the blood sugar roller coaster.

Blood sugar in the form of glucose has a profound impact on our thinking and brain functioning. In fact, 80% of all blood sugar is used by the brain. When the level is stable, our thinking is level-headed. Our brains are optimally fuelled. We are more intentional, make better decisions and feel more alert – our resilient best selves can show up.

When it dips, we experience fatigue, irritability ('hanger'), anxiety and impulsivity. Self-control takes a back seat. Not helpful for courageous decision making.

What we put in our mouths determines our blood sugar levels. Don't make the mistake (as I used to, somewhat smugly) of thinking this is just a matter of how much actual sugar is in our food. *All* carbohydrates (including alcohol) are converted into sugar in the body. The problem arises when the carbohydrates are highly processed or refined (think white flour, bread, pastries, pasta, sugar, cookies, most breakfast cereals). They're digested super fast, resulting in a sudden and dangerous blood sugar tsunami. From your body's perspective, this counts as a metabolic crisis. Insulin is released quickly to lower the toxic levels. This works too well, and blood sugar levels then drop to below normal levels – your brain stops working so well, and your memory, energy and mood suffer. Your evil twin shows up. You may experience a powerful urge to eat something sweet. Now. And back up the roller coaster you go.

There's plenty of evidence that fast-digesting carbohydrates, fun though they are, undermine thinking. David Ludwig, professor and researcher at Harvard Medical School, is one of the world's leading researchers on optimal nutrition. He describes intriguing research demonstrating the impact of slow- versus fast-digesting carbohydrates:

In a carefully controlled feeding study, researchers from the University of Wales in the United Kingdom gave seventy-one female undergraduate students slow- or fast-digesting carbohydrate-based breakfasts and then tested their cognitive functioning. They found that memory, especially for hard words, was impaired throughout the morning after the fast-digesting breakfast. This effect was most pronounced several hours after the meal (a 33% deficit). Similar results were obtained in Toronto among twenty-one patients with diabetes. Following a meal with fast-digesting carbohydrate, verbal memory performance, working memory, selective attention, and executive function were worse compared to a meal containing the same amount of carbohydrate in slow-digesting form.

So what sort of foods will release energy slowly to keep our minds working well for longer? We could begin with Michael Pollan's seven-word guidance for eating well:

'*Eat food. Not too much. Mostly plants.*'

By 'food' he means 'real food', not industrially processed food-like material. Unfortunately, much of what lines supermarket shelves today fails this test. Michael has a number of rules for avoiding junk food. They include:

- Don't eat anything your grandmother wouldn't recognise as food.

- Avoid food products containing ingredients that are a) unfamiliar, b) unpronounceable, c) more than five in number, or that include d) high-fructose corn syrup.

- Avoid foods that make health claims.

- Get out of the supermarket whenever possible (and shop at farmers' markets).

- Don't get your fuel from the same place your car does.

The onus is on us to choose wisely. Supermarkets are not our friends. Friends don't poison you slowly.

The scientifically oriented among you may delight in looking up the glycemic index (GI) for different foods – this is a measure of how quickly food releases glucose into the blood stream. Some foods, such as meat, eggs, fish, avocado and most vegetables, have such minimal amounts of carbohydrate that they don't even have a GI value. Higher GI foods include mashed potato (83), white bread (70), wholemeal bread (70) and pizza (80). I love them too (sob).

An excellent source of information is the international GI database maintained by the University of Sydney at www.glycemicindex.com. They offer the very sound (and achievable) advice that we should aim to have at least one-low GI food with every meal. That sounds doable to me.

REEF RESILIENCE

Astronauts looking back at Earth frequently report a life-changing shift in perspective. Buzz Aldrin described our planet as 'a brilliant jewel in the black velvet sky'. It's not until we step back and see the bigger picture that a profound sense of awe, interconnection and appreciation becomes fully possible. One of the things astronauts see from space is the Great Barrier Reef stretching over 2300 kilometres off the north-east coast of Australia. It's the world's biggest single structure made by living organisms.

The Great Barrier Reef may look like one thing from a distance, but up close it's an incredible interconnected system of 2900 individual reefs built of 400 coral species. The coral provides a home to 1500 fish species, over 5000 types of molluscs, 500 kinds of seaweed, 125 species of shark, 30 different whales, 17 species of sea snake and six kinds of frog. None of these species live in isolation – they need and depend on each other for food, shelter, defence, transport, and sometimes even to clean one another. The coral needs the life around it. The life around it needs the coral. It's a resilient system because of its diversity. Reduce the diversity, and the reef becomes less healthy.

Unfortunately, the reef has lost more than half of its coral cover since 1985. The resilience of the system has been eroded and it's vulnerable to accelerated destruction. One of the main contributors to reef destruction is the coral-hungry crown-of-thorns starfish. It's been a royal pain in the reef. Reefs can tolerate small numbers of these starfish, but numbers have exploded in recent years. The reason is excessive fertiliser runoff from agriculture which feeds algae which in turn feeds the starfish. Which then go on to consume and destroy the reef. Unnatural levels of nutrients have destabilised an otherwise resilient system.

ONLY 50% HUMAN

Stand back from a human being and it looks, well, like one thing. But when we take a closer look we can see that's not the case at all: 50% of the living cells in a person aren't actually human at all. It's estimated we each have around 38 trillion bacteria in our gut, composed of about 500 species. Not only bacteria, but viruses and yeasts too. Together these microbes make up the microbiome, a cosmopolitan community together weighing somewhere between one and three kilograms. These aren't passive passengers hitching a lift. They are active and critical participants in human life. We need them and they need us. Way back in our evolution a deal was struck. In return for a little food and shelter, friendly microbes would fight off unfriendly microbes, the pathogens. To sweeten the deal, friendly microbes also agreed to throw in an agreement to create vitamins that we cannot, heal the gut wall, reduce inflammation, stress, anxiety and depression, and improve mood, memory and resilience to emotional challenges. We said yes.

The connection between the gut and our health has long been recognised. As long ago as 400 BC Hippocrates, the father of medicine himself is claimed to have said: 'Let food be thy medicine and medicine be thy food.' The puzzle as to quite how this worked began to be revealed early in the 19th century when Élie Metchnikoff, the Russian Nobel Prize winning immunology researcher, pointed to yoghurt as a source of friendly microbes to restore a healthy balance to gut flora. Research has continued ever since. But it's only in the last few years that we've begun to get some inkling of the astonishing extent to which the life in our gut impacts our minds, moods and feelings.

Researchers such as John Cryan, chair of Anatomy and Neuroscience, and Ted Dinan, head of the Department of Psychiatry, both at University College Cork, Ireland, are revolutionising our understanding of psychobiotics – the microbes that improve our mood.

How on earth do microbes achieve this? It's now known they create significant amounts of neurotransmitters such as serotonin, dopamine and GABA, chemicals which influence whether you feel depressed, anxious or happy. Microbes don't have brains or neurones, so why create them? Because you do. The entire length of the human gut is wrapped up in a neuronal network which has been named the 'second brain'. It handles digestion automatically so you don't have to think about it. This second brain is connected to the brain in your head by the vagus nerve. It's not fully understood how, but different bacteria in the gut appear to send different messages to our brain via the vagus nerve, such as:

- 'Feed us!'

- 'Send more carbohydrates!'

- 'Send sugar!'

- 'Send protein!'

When you have a craving for something (you know what I'm talking about), it may not originally have been *your* craving at all. When you feed the microbes what they like, they send rewarding messages back.

When I met Professor Cryan at the IPPA Sixth Positive Psychology World Congress in Melbourne in 2019, he described how people suffering from anxiety and depression often have a microbiome with diminished diversity. One way the life in our inner reef can get out of whack is by inundating it with excessive nutrient runoff, say by continually grazing on foods rich in sugar and flour. Health can be restored by choosing foods that are healthy for ourselves *and* our inner friends.

For a more detailed exploration of the new science of the gut–brain connection and recommendations for taking care of your gut health, have a look at *The Psychobiotic Revolution* by Scott Anderson, John Cryan and Ted Dinan. Here are a few of the book's suggestions for improving your gut health:

- **Eat more vegetables.** This helps on multiple levels. Not only are vegetables directly nutritious but friendly gut microbes digest the fibre and create butyric acid as a by-product. Butyric acid is a superfuel for the cells lining your gut, helping to rebuild your lining. Butyric acid can also promote the production of feel-good neurotransmitters. As a bonus, vegetables contain probiotics in addition to prebiotics. Vegetables especially loved by 'good' bacteria include:

  - artichokes
  - chicory
  - lentils
  - asparagus
  - beans
  - onions

- garlic
- leeks
- bananas (yes, bananas can be classed as vegetables)
- beets
- broccoli.

- **Eat live yogurt.** A 2013 study[1] using brain scanners showed that healthy women who ate a yogurt containing a standard mix of probiotics for four weeks had enhanced activity in the parts of the brain processing emotion and sensation, which corresponded to an improvement in mood. This study demonstrated that probiotics are also helpful for otherwise healthy people.

- **Eat fermented and pickled foods** such as sauerkraut, kimchi, miso and kombucha.

- **Drop the junk food.** Processed meats; anything made with white flour; sugar; sweets; potato chips. You know this already. Large studies show a strong connection between junk food and anxiety and depression. It seems very likely a compromised gut biota is a significant contributor.

- **Eat a diverse diet** of vegetables, fruits, fish, high-fibre grains, nuts and eggs. None of this will come as a surprise (hopefully). The nutritious diet we've been long encouraged to eat for our health is also healthy for our gut biome. Which in turn is good for us.

- **Get plenty of omega-3 fats.** Fish such as sardines, salmon, trout, tuna and cod are especially good sources, although they can also be found in olives, nuts and soybeans.

---

1   Tillisch K, Labus J, et al. 'Consumption of Fermented Milk Product With Probiotic Modulates Brain Activity.' *Gastroenterology*, https://doi.org/10.1053/j.gastro.2013.02.043.

- **Drink less alcohol.** It disrupts the balance of microbiota and increases the permeability of the gut to toxins. Sorry.

- **Exercise.** Your gut biome loves it when you move. Any exercise counts. Just move.

- **Don't eat.** Intermittent fasting – increasing the length of time you don't eat each day – isn't just good for losing a little weight. It also improves gut health. We all stop eating while we're asleep, and extending this period to 12 or more hours can also contribute to a healthier gut biome.

What, how and when we eat profoundly impacts our mood, thinking, energy and resilience. Our ability to live courageously is significantly impacted by how we nourish ourselves and the ecosystem we live with.

READING AND VIEWING

- Anderson, Scott, John Cryan, and Ted Dinan. *The Psychobiotic Revolution: Mood, food, and the new science of the gut–brain connection.* National Geographic, 2017.

- Ludwig, David and Dawn Ludwig. *Always Hungry? Conquer cravings, retrain your fat cells, and lose weight permanently.* Grand Central Publishing, 2018.

- *Apollo 11.* Directed by Todd Douglas Miller. 2019.

- Pollan, Michael. *In Defense of Food: An eater's manifesto.* Penguin Books, 2009.

- University of Sydney. *Glycemic Index.* www.glycemicindex.com.

- Taubes, Gary. *Why We Get Fat: And what to do about it.* Anchor, 2011.

CHAPTER SUMMARY

- The proliferation of the Western diet around the world over the last 50 years is correlated with increases in Western diseases such as diabetes, cancer and heart disease. It's also correlated with greater anxiety and depression.

- Our mood and thinking are directly impacted by what, how and when we eat.

- Slow-digesting carbohydrates release energy slowly, fuelling improved moods and thinking.

- Fast-digesting carbohydrates release energy quickly and put us on a blood sugar roller coaster.

- We are not individual creatures – a human being is a cosmopolitan community of billions. Your mood is significantly influenced by your gut health and microbiome diversity.

Part III

STANCES TO EMBOLDEN

'If you change the way you look at things,
the things you look at change.'

WAYNE DYER

When I relocated to Munich to work with Motorola I was committed to enjoying the experience. Munich is a marvellous city with a historical centre located just half an hour from the Alps – a playground for people who love snow sports, biking, hiking and drinking good beer afterwards. Germans are very enthusiastic about having fun outdoors. They know what they're doing.

To make the most of the snow I decided to learn how to snowboard. Mistake. I'd assumed that surfing snow, which looked so fun and cool, would be much easier than skiing, which to my eyes looked ungainly and treacherous. Wrong.

Learning was slow and painful. It turns out that when two legs are stuck to one board you are less stable than when two legs are stuck to two skis. I fell – a lot. Before falling less. And then rarely.

But during my slow learning journey there was one particular section on a long easy run where I fell repeatedly. There was a low bump which crossed the piste. Roads sometimes have similar bumps to slow traffic. I could see this bump approaching, and it didn't seem to matter how ready I was, I would fall. Every time. I tried going slow. I fell. I tried going fast. I fell. I tried crossing at an angle. I fell. It took an embarrassingly long time, but I finally worked out how to elegantly get over the bump with almost no effort whatsoever. I adjusted my stance. All I needed to do was squat a little, get lower to the ground and allow my knees to bend as I hit the inevitable bump. It had an instant, magical effect. Not only was I over the bump upright, but suddenly I could explore other bumpy sections of the ski slopes that had previously been off limits for me. This small adjustment to my stance gave me flexibility and resilience. With no extra effort.

All sports require different stances to play well under different circumstances. Golfers adjust their stance to play from the tee, in bunkers, on slopes and on the greens. Tennis players adjust their stance to deliver or receive a serve. And weight lifters optimise their performance by adopting a stance that will give them the strongest foundation to execute the techniques they've practised. Whatever the sport, an optimal stance minimises effort and maximises performance.

Sports professionals also understand that in addition to the outer game, there is an inner game. Timothy Gallwey, author of *The Inner Game of Tennis* and widely acknowledged as the godfather of coaching, describes the importance of the inner game as follows: 'The player of the inner game comes to value the art of relaxed concentration above all other skills; he discovers a true basis for self-confidence; and he learns that the secret to winning any game lies in not trying too hard.'

We are all playing the game of life. There's an outer game of taking courageous actions. And an inner game of attitudes and mindsets. These mental stances provide an optimal foundation to play skilfully and with less effort.

In this part we will look at three mental stances to embolden us to play well allowing for the circumstances we find ourselves in – our human predicaments.

Chapter 7

DEFIANT GRATITUDE

'He is a wise man who does not grieve for the things
which he has not, but rejoices for those which he has.'

EPICTETUS

Acceptance, collaboration or resistance?

Which option would you choose if your country was invaded and occupied by a foreign power? The French population faced this terrible choice after German Nazi forces swiftly occupied Paris in June 1940. Now there were swastikas hanging from the Eiffel Tower. The new order demanded compliance – disobedience was to be swiftly punished. Increasingly severe conditions were imposed on the French nation – censorship, incessant propaganda, night curfews, the devaluation of the French currency by 20%, food requisition, rationing, malnutrition and hunger, forced labour, and – incredibly – they had to pay for their own occupation! Astonishing as it sounds, the French were obliged to pay for upkeep of the 300,000 German soldiers now stationed in France – a cost equivalent to 400 million French francs a day. Surrender came with terrible costs.

The French Resistance movement that arose exemplified courageous defiance. Despite the threat of execution and brutal reprisals, a small number of individuals from all walks of life and political persuasions refused to submit to Nazi control. They took to heart Napoleon's words that 'Death is nothing, but to live defeated and inglorious is to die daily'. They would not surrender to tyrannical control. They demanded back their freedom to live as they chose, not as others dictated.

Exceptionally brave women and men printed underground newspapers, and sabotaged the electrical power grid, transport facilities and telecommunications networks. They tore down propaganda posters and maintained escape networks for Allied soldiers and airmen trapped behind enemy lines. They provided invaluable intelligence on the location and strength of German forces to 'Churchill's Secret Army', the British Special Operations Executive. This information was invaluable during the Allied Normandy landings. It took four years, but in June 1944 the Allies – supported by the French Resistance – forced the

Germans to retreat from France. Liberation was finally achieved. The French nation could lead lives true to their own values once more.

THE PRICE OF SURRENDERING TO HUMAN PREDICAMENTS

The circumstances the French faced in 1940 are very different to our own. However, a defiant attitude to our own predicaments also empowers us to achieve a different kind of liberation. A liberation to live more to our own choosing, and not be dictated to by others.

Let's review some of the costs of surrendering to our human predicaments.

HUMAN PREDICAMENTS	COMBINED COSTS
We live in two worlds – real and imagined: • our negativity bias impacts both worlds • by default, our thinking is often fearful • we are quick to imagine dragons and spend much of our lives avoiding non-existent threats.	We surrender living personally meaningful lives. We obediently invest finite life energies in building the pyramids of others. We squander precious minutes as though we will live forever. We play life defensively. We avoid challenges that lead to greater personal and professional achievement. We live safer, smaller and more timid lives.

HUMAN PREDICAMENTS	COMBINED COSTS
We're drip-fed junk values that exploit our negativity bias. Society tells us: • normal people are always happy • to prioritise immediate pleasure • discomfort is bad • we are not enough and do not have enough. Fix it with more. Do not stop • wellbeing comes from having more to impress others. We can never have enough • relentless positivity is approved. Difficult experiences are unwelcome. **We know we will die:** • we are unwilling to really accept our unacceptable, certain demise • we self-soothe through avoidance, distraction, numbing and denial • as a result, we undervalue that which is most precious • we deny ourselves an appreciative urgency to fuel courageous living.	We conform and suppress our own thoughts, tastes and identities. We abdicate self-leadership. We chase satisfaction in hamster wheels of futility that generate energy for self-interested organisations. Our over-avoidance of negativity and vulnerability diminishes relationships and courageous action. We cage our own potential: • to live courageously • to learn, grow and develop • to improve the quality of life for ourselves, for others and the planet. We share the top regret of the dying: I wish I'd had the courage to live a life true to myself, not the life others expected of me.

DEFIANCE NOT COMPLIANCE

Assuming the costs of junk value compliance are unacceptable, what can we do about it? We've already discussed how we can get fit for purpose through good sleep, exercise and nutrition. However, we can't change our fundamental genetic make-up, and the broader culture of consumerism has enormous inertia to change. How can we play well regardless?

I propose that the first stance for playing the game of courageous living optimally is one of **defiant gratitude** in the face of our circumstances. It's defiant in the sense that we can choose not to allow toxic elements of our culture, nor allow our mortality to crush our spirits. Instead, with radical honesty we can recognise our situation *and* decide to live more wholeheartedly *because of it*.

In this chapter, we'll explore how gratitude is both an antidote to many of our human predicaments and a bold act of intentional defiance.

GRATITUDE

Ancient wisdom from philosophy and religion has long endorsed gratitude as an approach to leading happier and more fulfilled lives. Considerable recent scientific research agrees. Gratitude – thankfulness for something beneficial received – is much more than a temporary pleasant feeling. It has profound, enduring consequences on our physical and mental health, and changes how we engage with life. It emboldens us.

Robert Emmons, the world's leading scientific expert on gratitude and author of *Thanks!: How the new science of gratitude can make you happier*, emphasises that gratitude isn't about plastering over the cracks in life with a pervasive Pollyanna positivity. He sees it as a more honest approach to living, acknowledging the good that exists *in addition* to the bad: 'This doesn't mean that life is perfect; it doesn't ignore complaints, burdens, and hassles. But when we look at life as a whole, gratitude encourages us to identify some amount of goodness in our life.'

Research conducted by Emmons and others has shown that regularly experiencing gratitude has transformative effects on our bodies, minds and relationships:

Bodies:

- We sleep longer and feel more refreshed.
- We enjoy stronger immune systems.
- We have lower blood pressure.

Minds:

- We are happier.
- We are more optimistic.
- We experience less stress and more resilience.

Relationships:

- We are less lonely and isolated.
- We experience a greater sense of belonging and connectedness.
- We are more helpful and collaborative.
- We are more outgoing.

LONG-TERM BENEFITS FROM BRIEF EXPERIENCES

Barbara Frederickson, professor of psychology at the University of North Carolina at Chapel Hill, has dedicated her life to researching the impacts of positive emotions. She says that while negative emotions narrow our thinking and behaviours, making us more reactive and inflexible, positive emotions do the opposite. They broaden our thinking and open our options for action. We become more creative, proactive and flexible. We become less defensive and open to life. As a consequence, we're emboldened to build experiences, relationships, skills and learning. She says:

> Through experiences of positive emotions, individuals can transform themselves, becoming more creative, knowledgeable, resilient, socially integrated, and healthy. Individuals who regularly experience positive emotions, then, are not stagnant. Instead, they continually grow toward optimal functioning. How is this continued growth sustained? Positive emotions provide the fuel, creating a self-sustaining system. In particular, positive emotions generate what I have called an upward spiral toward optimal functioning and enhanced emotional wellbeing.

Frederickson thinks the practice of gratitude might also work as an antidote to the lingering after-effects of negative emotions. In contrast to those, gratitude produces a cascade of beneficial outcomes, including more friendly and prosocial behaviour, a greater sense of belonging, feeling supported and valued, and an improved sense of self-worth.

A greater sense of self-worth from social connections and a greater valuing of what we already have in life combine to create a buffer against toxic cultural messages that we are 'not enough'. Our identities are shaped by the memories we collect. Emmons describes the important role gratitude has in shaping our identities like this:

> One could even say that we are because of what we remember. Gratitude is the way the heart remembers – remembers kindnesses, cherished interactions with others, compassionate actions of strangers, surprise gifts, and everyday blessings. By remembering we honour and acknowledge the many ways in which who and what we are has been shaped by others, both living and dead.

WHAT UNDERMINES GRATITUDE?

If gratitude is so unrelentingly happiness-inducing, reducing stressful reactivity and boosting courageous living, why aren't we all already doing it?

There are a number of reasons:

- **Our negativity bias tilts attention towards what's bad.** When we're on autopilot we're more likely to notice what's missing. This is exacerbated when we're tired, stressed or rushed. Gratitude requires intentionally pausing to notice what's good, savouring the gift and appreciating the giver (for example, a person, a group, nature, the cosmos, luck, a supreme being if you hold such beliefs).

- **It's effortful.** Emmons even says 'it is not for the intellectually lethargic!' On the upside, we get better at what we practise. The brain adapts. This isn't restricted to playing music, sport or Candy Crush. It also applies to habits of thought. Practise gratitude and you rewire your brain for good, noticing more good stuff with less effort. You can counteract the negativity bias to level the playing field. A habitual orientation of gratitude transforms your experience of life. You'll get more joy out of everything. Gratitude is a joy juicer. It's a Nutribullet for good experiences and circumstances.

- **We take the familiar for granted.** We're excited by the shiny and new. But not for long. New becomes normal astonishingly quickly. We can habituate to anything. Anything? Yes, even winning the lottery. Research published in the *Journal of Personality and Social Psychology* found that 22 lottery winners were no happier after their win and actually took *less* pleasure out of simple things. Gratitude inoculates you against taking any good fortune for granted. A life stance of gratitude will prepare you to really make the most out of that next lottery win! And even if you don't win, your experience of being alive will be considerably enriched. So, you win either way.

- **We feel entitled and deserving.** Why be thankful when our good circumstances are entirely due to our own efforts or superiority? This perspective can only be propped up by taking full responsibility for the totality of one's circumstances and dismissing as negligible the contributions of others and chance.

  Such arrogance requires taking personal credit for our:

  - genetic make-up
  - upbringing
  - education
  - culture
  - language
  - food
  - environment
  - access to services developed and maintained by others, such as electricity, the internet, water, healthcare, roads, air travel, all books ever written, all knowledge and discoveries gathered over history by the efforts of others, all science and art
  - nature
  - sunshine
  - air
  - the moon, the sun and stars
  - gravity, the seasons, and the laws of physics
  - life.

Gratitude does not require surrendering deserved pride for the smart choices you've made. However, each of us is also the beneficiary of considerable good fortune and the contributions of others, seen and unseen, alive and dead. We are all interdependent. One of the smartest choices we can make is to be thankful for that.

- **We worry that gratitude will undermine our drive and ambition.** I get this. Won't satisfaction deplete our motivation? The research says no, quite the opposite. A 10-week study by Emmons and McCulloch asked participants divided into three groups to write down just five things each week. The first group wrote about things they were grateful or thankful for, the second group wrote about hassles, the third group wrote about neutral life events. The gratitude group made 20% more progress towards important personal goals. They were also more optimistic and felt better about their lives as a whole.

Emmons says that grateful people are mindful materialists. They want and enjoy what they already have but this doesn't stop them from happily striving towards achieving more.

THE RIPPLE EFFECT OF GRATITUDE

The benefits of gratitude touch lives broadly and profoundly. Emmons summarises the benefits of gratitude as follows:

> *Specifically, we have shown that gratitude is positively related to such critical outcomes as life satisfaction, vitality, happiness, self-esteem, optimism, hope, empathy, and the willingness to provide emotional and tangible support for other people, whereas being ungrateful is related to anxiety, depression, envy, materialism, and loneliness. Collectively, such studies present credible evidence that feeling grateful*

generates a ripple effect through every area of our lives, potentially satisfying some of our deepest yearnings – our desire for happiness, our pursuit of better relationships, and our ceaseless quest for inner peace, wholeness, and contentment.

On top of everything else, it's free.

DEVELOPING AN ATTITUDE OF GRATITUDE

Here's something else we can be grateful for – developing gratitude can be achieved with brief exercises, which you can do daily or weekly.

Daily journaling

It's quick, inexpensive and proven to work. Simply grab a pen and paper, and write down what you're thankful for. You don't need to write an essay; a few sentences will do. Don't worry about spelling and grammar, simply jot down one or more good things you've experienced or have in your life. What is it you appreciate about that? Who or what contributed to this goodness coming into your life?

You can do this exercise in the morning or night – the timing doesn't matter (I do both, although experiencing gratitude before bed will improve sleep). You can do it once a week or daily – or whatever works for you. The objective is to activate the feeling of gratitude through writing. You can ignite gratitude by recalling what's good and appreciating both the benefit *and* the giver. Emmons says gratitude is amplified by thinking of the benefit as a gift. Sometimes good things come your way without there being an obvious giver. Thank life, or nature, or fortune, or God. Whatever feels appropriate to you.

Does it matter what you write with or on? Janice Kaplan, author of *The Gratitude Diaries: How a year of living gratefully changed my life*, recommends making a purposeful purchase of an attractive journal, something worthy of all the good things you'll be putting inside. Your journal becomes a treasure chest of lifetime goodness. You could get a nice new pen while you're at it.

Of course, you could write into your smartphone or computer. Or the UC Berkeley Greater Good Science Centre provides a free online gratitude journal at thnx4.org. There are plenty of journalling apps with free versions such as Day One, Diario and Journey. One of the upsides of using an app is you can include images with the text. There's research suggesting that taking photos of what you appreciate can boost your experience of gratitude.

To get the most out of a daily journal, don't let it become a chore. Grudgingly writing the same things like a resentful child instructed to count their blessings does not induce gratitude! Keep it fresh, and don't feel obliged to consistently come up with a set number of gratitude targets. One juicy thing is enough. It's the taste of gratitude that matters most.

Gratitude during adversity

Paradoxically, bad times can sometimes make it easier to experience gratitude than the good times. We all take what's familiar for granted. Adversity and loss serve as a wake-up call to remind us of a) the value of what we had, b) the value of what we still have, and c) our interdependence. We can be grateful for all three even as we regret the adversity itself.

I experienced this when I broke my leg, as I describe in the acknowl-edgements at the start of this book. The loss of mobility for three months made me hugely appreciative of the health I still had, the mobility I had enjoyed prior, and the people who were providing me with care. (Thank you, thank you, thank you.)

Post-traumatic growth

Awful things happen in life. Any good things that might also eventuate because of this do not make everything okay. It's *not* good to be hurt, robbed, betrayed, attacked or to get seriously ill. And yet, often, at the same time, good things do emerge. We make discoveries about others and ourselves. We are reminded of what matters. Adversity can be a potent fuel for personal growth and reorienting life in meaningful directions.

Gratitude for life

The imperial Roman Stoic philosopher Seneca recognised 2000 years ago that most of us overlook the priceless value of our most precious and irreplaceable resource – our time:

> *You are living as if destined to live for ever; your own frailty never occurs to you; you don't notice how much time has already passed, but squander it as though you had a full and overflowing supply.*

With our modern, busy, distracted lifestyles, it's easier than ever to keep mortality semi-comfortably out of mind and procrastinate our lives away as a consequence.

You have weeks to live

Must we wait for a terminal diagnosis before we can truly value life and ignite a fierce purpose to live well?

Seneca knew the solution lay in somehow making our remaining time visible:

> *But if each of us could have the tally of his future years set before him, as we can of our past years, how alarmed would be those who saw only a few years ahead, and how carefully would they use them!*

Seneca's solution would certainly be alarming. I'd prefer not to see how much time I actually have left. But there *is* value in making an estimate of our remaining time visible. The reality, of course, is that even without a terminal diagnosis, each of us already only has weeks to live. We just don't know how many.

You can get a graphic of your expected remaining weeks by visiting www.count.life. After entering your birthdate and life expectancy, you're shown a visualisation of the weeks of your entire life – the ones you've lived, and the ones you have left.

Here's mine, assuming I reach 85.

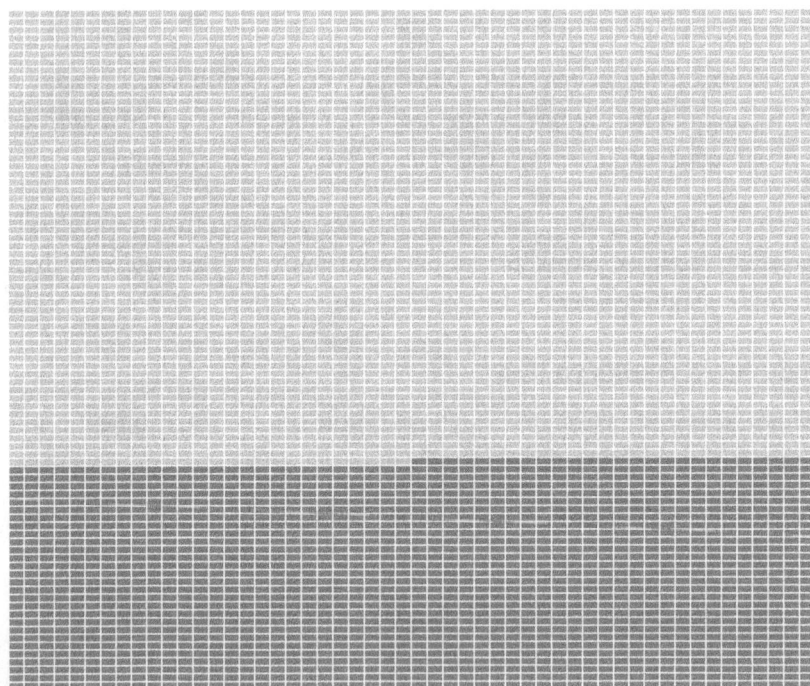

Quite startling, isn't it? I strongly encourage you to visit this website right now.

What is your experience of seeing your remaining weeks laid out? When I look at my own table, I'm struck by how short an 85-year life actually is when shown in weeks. Every unlived week is full of potential, and I feel a sense of urgency to make them all count. I've saved a bookmark for this webpage and I look at it every week. I've found this to be a very helpful way of boosting my appreciation of my time alive; it spurs me on to live with courage while I can.

'When you arise in the morning, think of what a precious privilege it is to be alive – to breathe, to think, to enjoy, to love.'

MARCUS AURELIUS

READING

- Count Life. www.count.life.

- Greater Good Science Centre. THNX4. www.thnx4.org.

- Emmons, Robert A. *Thanks!: How the new science of gratitude can make you happier.* New York: Houghton Mifflin Harcourt, 2007.

- Frederickson, Barbara. 'Gratitude, Like Other Positive Emotions, Broadens and Builds'. Robert Emmons and Michael McCullough (eds). *The Psychology of Gratitude.* Oxford University Press, 2004.

- Kaplan, Janice. *The Gratitude Diaries: how a year of looking on the bright side can transform your life.* Dutton, 2016.

- 'Lottery Winners and Accident Victims: Is happiness relative?' Brickman, Philip, Coates, Dan and Janoff-Bulman, Ronnie. *Journal of Personality and Social Psychology,* 1978, Vol. 36.

CHAPTER SUMMARY

- Surrendering to our human predicaments comes at a high price.

- Gratitude is a defiant and enabling stance in the face of our predicaments.

- Gratitude is developed by noticing what's valued and feeling thankful, in good times and bad times.

- Gratitude supports living a life true to yourself by reducing stress, anxiety and isolation, and boosting resilience, wellbeing and connectedness.

- Gratitude is an antidote to neediness promoted by our consumer culture.

- Gratitude for life left activates courage and purpose.

Chapter 8

SELF-COMPASSION

'Self-compassion inspires us to pursue
our dreams and creates the brave, confident,
curious, and resilient mind-set that allows us
to actually achieve them.'

KRISTIN NEFF

Ahh, the delicious joy of surprising discoveries. In the late 1990s I moved to Munich in the southern German 'free state' of Bavaria. Non-Bavarian Germans delighted in telling me Bavaria is called the free state because it's the only place Bavarians were allowed to run free. And they did. At the merest suggestion of good weather they ran, hiked and biked freely. Locals of all ages yearned to be outside having fun, exercising or perhaps recovering in one of the 180 beer gardens scattered across the city. Originally from England, when I think of a beer garden my mind conjures up an image of a few small tables on a tatty lawn out the back of a pub. Pleasant enough, but often difficult to get a table. The Germans have fully developed the Biergarten concept. The typical location is public parkland. The tables are long, hefty wooden constructions under trees, providing generous communal seating. Munich's largest Biergarten, the Hirschgarten, has room for a whopping 8000 people. Large or small, Biergartens are delightful places where you can bring your own food and enjoy the world's greatest beer during the day, or ideally, late into a warm summer evening. Prost!

Before arriving in Munich I had been working as an IT specialist for IBM in Edinburgh and Abu Dhabi. My problem-solving mind delighted in puzzling out technical challenges, designing data protection systems and training others how to operate them. The pace was fast, technology was constantly changing, deadlines were tight, there was always lots to learn and much at stake. The pressure was on.

I loved it, and thrived. At that time anyone with specialist IT skills had the freedom to live and work pretty much where they wanted. So I did. I enjoyed discovering new countries, cities and cultures. Whether in Scotland, England, the United Arab Emirates, the United States or Germany, my multicultural colleagues had different ways of seeing things and could be as certain of the rightness of their point of view as I was. It's been said that the world is divided up into people who think they are right. My observation is that it's mostly divided up into people who *know* they are right. Collaborating with people from diverse backgrounds certainly broadened my narrow UK perspective. I enjoyed a more flexible point of view, which helped me solve more problems and work with others more effectively.

During my time in Munich I began to develop an interest in how to manage the mind to improve motivation, performance and wellbeing. I'd attended one of Motivation Master Tony Robbins's three-day events on a trip to Toronto – the frenzied US-style of delivery was a little obnoxious to English sensibilities (and to more than a few Canadians too) but there was much that was intriguing about the whole thing. I learnt I had a lot more influence over my mind and behaviour than I had realised. My appetite for learning these skills was piqued.

If you had told me back then, perhaps over an impressively large, cold Munich beer on a steamy summer evening under the trees in a Biergarten, that you had learnt of an approach that built emotional intelligence, resilience *and* motivation, you would have had my full and eager attention. But had you uttered the word 'self-compassion' in the next sentence you would have lost me. I'd have stayed just long enough to finish my beer.

As a highly rational and logical corporate warrior I believed in manuals, mastery and making an effort. Stuff gets done with drive and mental toughness. If you haven't succeeded at something, try harder for longer. Self-compassion? Surely a wishy-washy recipe for self-indulgence, self-pity and complacency. You can keep your fluffy feel-goodery.

It wasn't until I met the world's leading researcher on self-compassion, Kristin Neff, that I wised up. Over two days in Sydney, Kristin explained misconceptions around self-compassion, described the three components which generate it, and presented extensive research demonstrating that it measurably boosts emotional intelligence, resilience, personal development and enduring motivation. She was even able to satisfy my appetite for science by demonstrating why it works at a biochemical level. Her wonderful book *Self-Compassion* went into even greater detail. I lapped it up. Phew … it's fluff-free after all!

This chapter describes the second stance for taking courageous actions: **self-compassion**. It's a counterintuitive antidote to many of our human predicaments. There are many things in life that you might not expect to work but do anyway. Spending energy gives us energy (exercise), doing less gets more done (taking breaks), sleeping for longer can make us much more effective, and doing one thing at a time is seriously more effective than multi-tasking for those more thinky tasks.

As already discussed, our hyper-comparative and hyper-individualistic culture encourages us to consider ourselves as lacking and personally responsible for our shortcomings, so that somebody can sell you the solution. Spend just a few minutes on social media, in a shopping mall or – worst of all – go through airport duty-free and you'll be quickly reminded that you're not enough as you are. (However, with the right watch, fragrance or cosmetics, you too can be successful, popular and irresistible!)

Failure to overcome your inadequacies – by not achieving Olympic levels of fitness, not being continually sexually alluring, not being more popular than everyone else, or a perfect parent, or financially independent by 30 – means that on top of everything else you are clearly also lacking self-control, willpower and talent. Good enough remains forever out of reach. You are not okay as you are. Now attempt to fill the gaps with purchases. Repeat.

For many, a consumer culture that relentlessly points out shortcomings merely reinforces what was learnt from parents. It's tragic to watch, but for some parents nothing their children do is ever good enough. Each effort to win parental love and approval is met with criticism and correction. The drawing doesn't look right, the music is off-key, school marks aren't 100%, and sit up straight for goodness sakes. Only perfect is satisfactory. Try harder. I guess such parents mean to build their children up, but well-meaning constant criticism tears them down and erodes self-confidence.

Critical parents or not, it's little wonder we're dissatisfied with ourselves. Intuition tells us what will really boost our motivation to fix embarrassing deficits is a powerful prescription of self-criticism. Take as needed until symptoms of not-enoughness disappear.

THE DARK SPIRAL OF SELF-CRITICISM

Self-criticism does work – to some extent. Otherwise we would never use it. Unfortunately, it's not nearly as effective as our intuition tells us it should be. Self-criticism is a self-generated threat. Succeed – or else! It activates the fight-or-flight system, and causes anxiety and fear of failure. We don't want that, so the idea goes that we'll buck up, do the work, avoid failure and be happy. Sounds logical. But it's not psycho-logical.

There *is* an important role for evaluation to assess how we're doing. But the danger lies in evaluating ourselves as good or bad, rather than evaluating our actions as effective or ineffective. One is crippling. The other is empowering.

People tend to perform more poorly if they feel they're being closely watched and judged. Imagine someone leaning over your shoulder and tut-tutting in your ear while you try to get something done. Well, you don't need an audience; you can achieve the same result by watching and judging yourself. It even works while you're alone!

Paradoxically, self-criticism actually promotes procrastination. That way, it's not *really* your fault if you don't succeed. You didn't have enough time. You're not to blame. Self-critical people (and this is all of us to some degree) are also less willing to take responsibility when they *do* have enough time. So motivated are they to avoid self-criticism that they'll refuse to take ownership for their actions and thereby avoid learning how to do better.

Perversely, the continual threat of self-criticism fuels a defensiveness that prevents us from accepting constructive feedback and actually getting better.

Finally, self-criticism also saps self-confidence and depletes your ability to take courageous actions. At its worst it fuels perfectionism – only flawless performance is satisfactory. Anything less means you are worthless.

We need a more emotionally intelligent way to motivate ourselves to make the changes we choose for ourselves.

Kristin's research indicates that self-compassion does just that. She defines it like this:

> *First, it requires self-kindness, that we be gentle and understanding with ourselves rather than harshly critical and judgmental. Second, it requires recognition of our common humanity, feeling connected with others in the experience of life rather than feeling isolated and alienated by our suffering. Third, it requires mindfulness – that we hold our experience in balanced awareness, rather than ignoring our pain or exaggerating it. We must achieve and combine these three essential elements in order to be truly self-compassionate.*

So self-compassion is a combination of self-kindness, acknowledging our shared predicaments and mindfulness, while being more honestly self-aware. Let's look at each in turn.

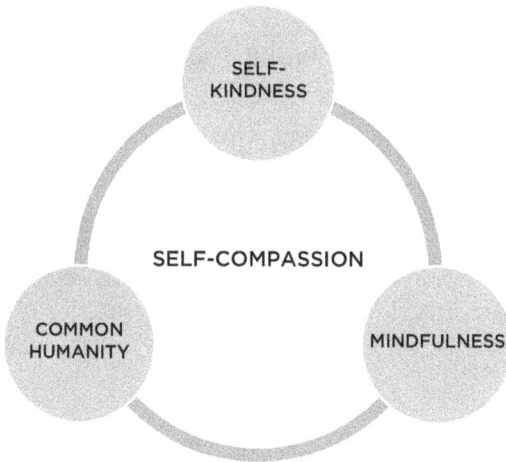

SELF-KINDNESS

Western culture promotes kindness to others in distress – it's highly valued socially and encouraged. Good thing too. But when it comes to ourselves, we're supposed to brush off personal distress and just get on with it. The phrase 'man up' says a great deal about what our culture expects from a socially approved man. He'll be emotion-lite, never show fear or display weakness. He's got a grip. This debilitating idea can also diminish women who may feel obliged to conform to stereotypical male behaviours when taking on leadership roles.

When we show self-kindness, we choose to actively comfort ourselves just as we would a friend in need. You deserve no less. When a friend is suffering we acknowledge their distress. We sit with them. Hear them. Validate what they're experiencing. We get it, and let them know we get it. Validation of difficult experiences soothes people and, most importantly, empowers them to take appropriate helpful actions. Validation is key.

Caring is fundamental to being human. Not merely a nice idea, it also has measurable impacts on the mind and body. When we give and receive care, the 'tend and befriend' system is activated. The hormone oxytocin is released – this happens whether we are cared for by another or if we are friendly and caring to ourselves. The brain can't tell the difference.

Oxytocin has a number of effects which work together to support courageous behaviour. It reduces:

- fear and anxiety

- the negativity bias

- reactivity and defensiveness.

It increases:

- a willingness to take risks

- emotional intelligence to maintain balance when challenged

- proactivity and courageous action.

A simple and discreet way to practise self-kindness when you're experiencing distressing thoughts or feelings is through touch. You can place a kind hand over your heart, or rest it on your arm, or give yourself a gentle hug. The experience of touch, even our own, soothes us. When combined with an attitude that says 'yes, this is challenging', you are validating your current experience.

You can also turn self-kindness towards self-critical thoughts. When a part of you pumps out such thoughts (in the mistaken belief that this is helpful) then you can hold that experience kindly too. No need to get into an argument with yourself. Instead, just validate the thought you are having: *Ahh, I'm having the thought that I'm no good.* This strategy honestly acknowledges the reality of your experience.

COMMON HUMANITY

The need to belong is woven into our core. Our ancestors discovered early on there is safety in belonging to a group. Together we could defend ourselves against predators and unfriendly tribes. Together we could hunt more effectively. Together we could combine our different skills, and share knowledge, support and protection.

Alone your chances were not so good. You are slow and good to eat. Isolation meant danger. Isolation is understandably anxiety provoking.

No wonder then that the experience of belonging is fundamental to our emotional health. Research shows that a sense of connection and belonging actually makes us resilient to life's challenges.

Introverts reading this may be dubious. You may be thinking, *hang on, I love my isolation thanks. I don't feel in the least bit anxious. Quite the opposite. I feel awesome by myself!*

I get it. I'm an introvert. I also restore my energy through time alone. However, introverts need a little connection too. I very much appreciate brief doses of company with one or two others. I especially like speaking to large audiences about emotional intelligence, resilience and courage. I enjoy running workshops. I spend energy with others gladly – but retire afterwards to recharge. We all need connection at times.

Social media and the prevailing positivity culture would have you believe everyone else is having a whale of a time. Smiling, laughing, travelling to exotic locations, continually thrilled to bits and succeeding where you are not. They are happy and they know it. But you don't feel like clapping your hands.

Our technology and culture amplifies a sense of isolation. It's all too easy to feel alone – to sense it's just you who is struggling with a sense of inadequacy, low worth, failure, doubt, anxiety. And even if you remove technology altogether, it's easy to confuse the cool exterior of another person with a cool interior. If we could only listen in to the crazily anxious thoughts of other people for a moment we might change our minds.

We're all in the same boat.

Although our prevailing culture encourages the idea you are personally responsible for your shortcomings, in actuality there are many factors that impact our circumstances, factors that mostly we do not choose. You did not choose your genetics, your family, your social history, the economy or the predominant cultural forces in play. We needn't take our 'personal failings' quite so personally.

We are self-compassionate when we kindly acknowledge that we are suffering, *just like everybody else*. This is what differentiates self-compassion from self-pity. You're not saying 'poor me'. You are recognising that anxiety, disappointment, setback, betrayal, humiliation and a host of other painful experiences are part of our shared humanity. It connects us.

MINDFULNESS

Neff describes mindfulness as 'holding our experience in balanced awareness, rather than ignoring our pain or exaggerating it.' I think of mindfulness as experiencing life honestly, without denial or wallowing. Saying yes to what is already present (whether we like it or not). Noticing without additional evaluation, experiencing without further interpretation.

We can be mindful of what's going on around us, in the outer world, and we can be mindful of what's happening in our inner world; that is, being self-aware. When we're mindfully self-aware we notice what we're telling ourselves, what we're feeling and thinking.

I have another confession. When I first heard about mindfulness meditation over 30 years ago, my mind conjured up images of chanting hippies sitting cross-legged in circles. I thought it had something to do with emptying the mind, or putting yourself into an ecstatic trance. I wasn't having a bar of it. I was seriously wrong, and it took another 15 years before I discovered what I'd been missing.

Mindfulness meditation, or mindfulness for short, is a form of attention training, a noticing skill with profoundly positive consequences. When you notice the story you're telling yourself or notice the emotions that arise then you interrupt mindless reactivity and defensiveness. You become less habitual and more intentional. It's a way of disengaging autopilot and taking ownership of your choices. Now you're the pilot and not the passenger.

You'll have noticed at times your negatively biased storytelling mind can transport you to some gloomy places. It's almost as though you're on a train of thought. We're carried away, reliving some past hurt, fantasising about what we should have said, what they would have done, how we would have responded, and then repeating it all over again.

Or instead we might gloomily predict an awful future. We just know how something will go badly, how we'll fail, be humiliated, end up destitute, unloved, nibbled by vermin in the gutter. And then we'll repeat the process. Once is never enough when you're catastrophising!

Mindfulness enables us to recognise when we're on a cognitive train of thought that'll take us somewhere unhelpful. It lets us step off, back onto the platform of the present moment. The train of thoughts and feelings is still there, but it no longer has the power to carry us away. Choice is restored. You can respond instead of react. You have more control over what you'll do next. It enables courageous actions.

Learning mindfulness skills has been the most positively impactful thing I've ever done. I used it initially to choose to drink less. I had got into a habit of drinking more than I really wanted and decided to dial it down. Funny thing was, I couldn't seem to do it. I kept putting it off. I tried using willpower. I tried keeping the stuff out of the house. I tried promising myself other rewards. Nothing seemed to work for long, until I learnt mindfulness. Then I could kindly notice the urges arising and choose not to drink. It's very liberating to discover you don't have to obey those inner dictators.

Part of our shared humanity is that at times we all experience unhelpful urges. The mind does not like feeling discomfort and will quickly initiate avoidance strategies such as:

- procrastinating
- avoiding difficult conversations
- being seen as right instead of, gasp, wrong!
- keeping quiet instead of risking disapproval
- conforming instead of expressing your individuality
- self-soothing with alcohol, food or other substances
- sulking to punish with silent disapproval.

This is of course an abridged list. You'll have your own entries.

Mindfulness skills give you an opportunity to catch yourself early, and consciously choose to act like the person you want to be. It won't make you a self-control master. But it will increase your self-influence.

You're being mindful anytime you notice what you're doing or saying to yourself. A simple exercise is to sit quietly and note your thoughts. You won't have to wait long before something shows up. One of your first thoughts might be along the lines of, *hmmm, nothing showing up yet.*

That'll do nicely. All you do is notice that thought and say 'thinking' in your head. No need to say it out loud. Then wait for the next one. Before long you'll be considering what you need to do later. You can note that with 'planning'. Maybe you'll recall something you did earlier. Note that with 'remembering'.

You'll discover that thoughts just arise by themselves. You cannot stop them showing up, but you can get better at recognising them and letting them go if they're unhelpful.

Mindfulness prevents fears from pushing you around, an essential skill in taking courageous actions.

To develop mindfulness skills, I can wholeheartedly recommend three apps: Waking Up, Headspace and Calm. Each will appeal to different personalities. I'm tempted to suggest what sort of people will prefer each app but I'm noticing the urge and I'm choosing to let you find out for yourself.

PUTTING IT TOGETHER

When feeling challenged, treat yourself as a valued friend going through a difficult experience. You are not alone; this is what it's like being human. Notice with kindness the train of thoughts and feelings and name them with kindness too. Be a friend to yourself.

Kristin Neff's website www.self-compassion.org has plenty of resources to learn more about this emboldening life stance.

I can also wholeheartedly recommend the free app 29k. Named after the average number of days in a human life, 29k is a non-profit based in Stockholm, Sweden. This organisation is on a mission to make personal growth available for everyone, for free. The app is the result of a collaboration between leading researchers and scientists from Harvard

University and the Karolinska Institute, one of the world's foremost medical universities. Take a look (29k.org).

READING, VIEWING AND LISTENING

- 'How to be kinder to yourself.' David, Susan. www.ideas.ted.com/how-to-be-kinder-to-yourself-self-compassion.

- 'Find Your Calm: Sleep more. Stress less. Live better'. www.calm.com.

- Harris, Sam. Waking Up. www.wakingup.com.

- Headspace. www.headspace.com.

- Neff, Kristin. Self-Compassion. www.self-compassion.org.

- Neff, Kristin. *Self-Compassion: The proven power of being kind to yourself*. William Morrow Paperbacks, 2015.

- 29k. www.29k.org.

CHAPTER SUMMARY

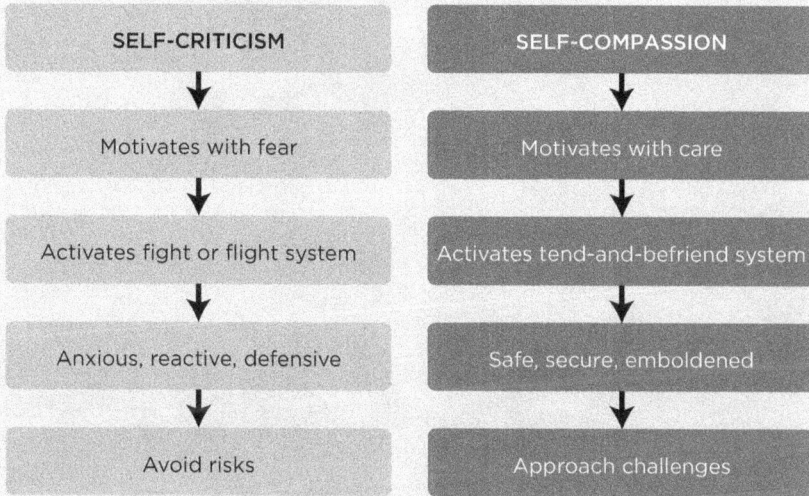

SELF-CRITICISM	SELF-COMPASSION
↓	↓
Motivates with fear	Motivates with care
↓	↓
Activates fight or flight system	Activates tend-and-befriend system
↓	↓
Anxious, reactive, defensive	Safe, secure, emboldened
↓	↓
Avoid risks	Approach challenges

Chapter 9

COURAGEOUS AUTHENTICITY

'Meaning is not something you stumble across,
like the answer to a riddle or the prize in a treasure hunt.
Meaning is something you build into your life.'

JOHN GARDNER

In an authentic existence we author our own lives. We take ownership of our precious time alive and decide what matters to us. And what doesn't. We decide what we'll accept for ourselves and others. And what we won't. We align our actions with what's personally important. We choose our own direction and how we'll show up along the way.

Not everyone is going to like it. At times, your choices will conflict with the traditions, values and expectations of:

- the culture you live in

- organisations you work in

- groups you belong to

- communities you live in

- your family of birth

- the family you create

- partners and spouses

- friends.

Living authentically sometimes means defying the expectations of others.

Three highly conspicuous examples of courageous authenticity are:

- **Greta Thunberg:** The Swedish climate change activist first challenged her parents to adopt lifestyle choices to reduce the family carbon footprint. She went on to protest outside the Swedish parliament by holding up a sign saying SKOLSTREJK FOR KLIMATET, which translates as SCHOOL STRIKE FOR THE CLIMATE. She has gone on to address the 2018 United Nations Climate Change Conference and the 2019 Climate Action Summit in New York. Her bold stand has inspired young and old around the world to change their own behaviour and demand more climate action from governments. *Time* magazine named her 2019 Person of the Year. Courageous authenticity doesn't get much more conspicuous than that.

- **Ayaan Hirsi Ali:** A Somali-born Dutch–American activist, feminist, and author of *Infidel* and *Heretic*, she is an outspoken advocate for the rights and self-determination of Muslim women, actively opposing female genital mutilation, forced marriages, 'honour' violence and child marriage. She is the founder of an organisation for the defence of all women's rights, the AHA Foundation.

- **Christian Picciolini:** At the age of 14 Christian joined a white supremacist group, ultimately becoming the leader of a violent hate group, the notorious Hammerskin Nation. He left the white power movement at 22 and co-founded Life After Hate, a non-profit organisation run by former extremists who are now dedicated to countering racism. In 2016 he won an Emmy for his role as director and executive producer of an anti-hate video campaign.

Courageous authenticity is, however, usually far less conspicuous. You take this stance every time you boldly do something that matters to you that risks failure, disapproval or rejection, such as:

- asking for what you want at work or in a relationship
- being seen and heard as yourself at work or in a relationship
- choosing not to follow the herd
- going back to school, college or university
- creating anything and showing it to others
- starting a conversation, relationship or job

- having a conversation, relationship or job
- concluding a conversation, relationship or job
- taking care of others
- taking care of yourself
- saying no to crossed boundaries
- challenging unfairness
- saying yes to opportunities
- dropping unhelpful habits
- establishing helpful habits
- initiating anything worthwhile.

'The easiest thing is to respond.
The second easiest thing is to react.
But the hardest thing is to initiate.'

SETH GODIN

Opportunities to be courageously authentic arise throughout every day. Well-lived lives are risky adventures.

Of course, none of us can be 100% authentic, all the time, in all circumstances. We all live, at times, in ways that do not represent our best selves. We procrastinate on personally important projects, we surrender to unhelpful urges to criticise or consume, we drink more than we mean to and consequently awake with less vitality for the next precious day.

And that's just me – you'll have your own list.

Equally, no one is totally inauthentic – all of us boldly choose, at times, to do what's right but hard. We live between the two poles on the authenticity continuum. However, we're not stuck. We can get better at noticing when we're off track and adjust our course. We can become more proactive about living with meaning. We can swipe right on our best selves more often.

Courageous authenticity is the third stance for living your life of daring adventure.

WHAT COURAGEOUS AUTHENTICITY *ISN'T*

Here are some things courageous authenticity is *not*:

- It's not blurting out exactly what's on your mind, yelling when your needs have been frustrated, or lashing out when you don't get your own way. Occasionally you'll find people proudly claiming that their unrestrained behaviour is just them being authentic. I've worked with people like this (which was bad) and dated someone like this (which was worse). Authenticity is intentionally choosing to take action aligned with enduring values, not abdicating self-control by reacting to fleeting feelings.

- It's not being reckless, inconsiderate or inflexibly indifferent to your situation. Just because you can do something, doesn't mean you should. We don't live in a vacuum – we each have responsibilities, duties and obligations to others as well as ourselves. Context matters. There are times when, considering the circumstances, it's wise to withhold your (doubtlessly correct but) contrary opinion or attend to the needs and preferences of others. Courageous authenticity is always mindful of the situation.

- It's not always being non-conformist. You may have decided to leave the herd of societal sheep obediently responding to advertising and cultural messaging regarding how you ought to fit in. However, your choices in life do not become authentic merely because they are the opposite of what the crowd are doing. Rebellious teenagers appalled at their parents' conformism may leave the family herd only to join another even more conspicuously conformist group, all adopting similar hairstyles, clothing and body language in a futile effort to be different.

A FEW WORDS ON COURAGE

We're courageous when we do what's personally important *and* challenging.

We're courageous when we do what matters *and* is difficult.

We're courageous when we prioritise meaning over comfort.

We talk about courage as though it's a thing. A thing that people get a certain amount of at birth. Some people seem to be naturally bold explorers from a young age, others are more cautious and risk avoidant. We do all have different natures, but courage isn't set in stone. In reality it's something that we do, it's a quality of action. It's a skill each of us can improve.

In her TED talk *The Gift and Power of Emotional Courage*, psychologist Susan David says: 'Courage is not an absence of fear; courage is fear walking.'

Fear walking. Walking right with you as you move in a direction that matters. Moving with meaning and experiencing vulnerability as you do so.

Brené Brown, research professor at the University of Houston, author of *Daring Greatly*, places vulnerability at the core of courageous living: 'You can choose courage or you can choose comfort, but you can't have both.' At the time of writing, her wonderful TED talk *The Power of Vulnerability* has over 45 million views, making it one of the most popular talks ever. Which means you've probably seen it. If not, stop reading and start watching – it's an excellent use of 20 minutes. And four seconds.

CHECK YOUR LADDER IS LEANING AGAINST THE RIGHT WALL

So what matters enough to us that we're willing to experience vulnerability? Many of the busy professionals I work with tell me they've been too busy to even think about it for long. Or sometimes ever. Instead, we climb ladders of success put up by our parents or by our culture. The view from the top and the cost of climbing may disappoint.

> 'If the ladder is not leaning against the right wall,
> every step we take just gets us to
> the wrong place faster.'
>
> **STEVEN COVEY**

There are a number of reasons why it's a good idea to reconfirm what matters to you:

- **The world is changing.** From today's perspective, many of the values we may have absorbed growing up are distasteful hand-me-downs. We can hand them back. I grew up in the 1970s watching *The Benny Hill Show*, an award-winning comedy on UK TV. Episodes consisted of a lecherous man stalking women, leering through windows or chasing them down the street. This didn't raise an eyebrow; in fact, it brought the house down!

- **Your circumstances change.** Priorities change as you move from partying teenager to young adult student, employed adult, responsible parent and irresponsible retiree. As we travel through different phases of life, different jobs and relationships, we inevitably change. Values may change or shift in terms of priority.

- **You change.** Your experiences throughout life change you. You develop and learn more about the world and what you care about. You outgrow some relationships, jobs and circumstances. You become wiser.

- **You make mistakes.** Inevitably some of the things we thought were important turned out not to be. You've trusted people who have betrayed that trust, you've pursued interests and passions that failed to live up to their potential.

A reassessment of what matters to you is worth doing annually.

WHAT DOES YOUR DEEPEST SELF CARE ABOUT?

'Men are not free when they are doing
just what they like. Men are only free when
they are doing what the deepest self likes.
And there is getting down to the deepest self!
It takes some diving.'

D. H. LAWRENCE

Working out what your personally meaningful life looks like requires some effort. When we don't choose what matters to us, others will. The junk values we soak up then masquerade as our own. We'll often confuse short-term pleasure with valued living. Identifying the ingredients of your personally meaningful life is an ongoing project of self-awareness.

There are many ways to identify what's personally meaningful to enable you to make authentic decisions as choices arise. We'll step through just a few of them here. Each of these is an exercise – that's to say, you can't dial up meaningful living by reading these instructions. You have to *follow* them. They deserve a little quiet time when your batteries are fully charged. These exercises work best if you write out the answers by hand, or if you prefer, type them out. But don't just think them through. There's a power in making thinking visual. Use it.

(The exercises in the rest of this chapter can be downloaded from www.ericwinters.com.au/swiperight-exercises.)

Starting and stopping

A part of you is probably already aware of what a more meaningful life would look like. So sit comfortably and write out the answers to these two questions:

- If there was one thing you could *start* doing right away, to make life more worthwhile, which one thing would make the biggest difference?

- If there was one thing you could *stop* doing right away to make your life more worthwhile, which one thing would make the biggest difference?

Areas, aims and actions

The following exercise has been adapted from an approach suggested by Rick Hanson, psychologist and *New York Times* bestselling author of *Resilient*, *Hardwiring Happiness* and *Buddha's Brain*. I've spent two weeks studying with Rick – he's an exceptional teacher with a passion for combining recent developments in neuroscience, positive psychology and mindfulness. He's created a highly practical approach to developing resilience, wellbeing and performance through brief and enjoyable daily practices. His books and online training at rickhanson.net are highly recommended.

First, make a list of the different areas in life – your high-level concerns. The following list is not meant to be conclusive, it's merely an example. Use your own words.

WORK
SPORT
KIDS
FAMILY
ENVIRONMENT
PLEASURE
CREATIVITY
FINANCE
SPIRITUAL LIFE
PARTNER
COMMUNITY
SELF-DEVELOPMENT
HEALTH

The areas you've listed are all important, but how would you prioritise them? It's understood that at times one area may require immediate attention. But all things being equal, how would you prioritise the areas of your life?

Write the names of each area on two separate post-its (or scraps of paper, or in a computer program where you'll be able to shuffle them around).[1] So you'll have two post-its each for FAMILY, two for HEALTH, and so on. Make two separate piles of your areas.

---

1   Incidentally, I like to use the laptop program Scapple for tasks like this. It's a simple tool for arranging ideas on a screen and moving them around. You'll find it at literatureandlatte.com. I use it for brainstorming ideas and developing my thinking daily.

Take one group and arrange the post-its in order of optimal priority by laying them on a table or sticking them on a wall, so you can see them. Maybe you'll put FAMILY on top, followed by WORK. Rearrange the list as you see fit. Give yourself time to consider what order makes most sense to you. Remember, you're not saying any of these are unimportant by placing them lower. They are just marginally less important.

Now that you can see your life areas prioritised, take that other pile of areas and arrange them in a way that represents how you have *actually* been prioritising them in your life over the last three months. You should end up with two lists looking something like this:

PRIORITY	
OPTIMAL	ACTUAL
KIDS	WORK
PARTNER	SPORT
HEALTH	KIDS
FINANCE	FAMILY
WORK	ENVIRONMENT
FAMILY	PLEASURE
SELF-DEVELOPMENT	CREATIVITY
PLEASURE	FINANCE
CREATIVITY	SPIRITUAL LIFE
SPORT	PARTNER
SPIRITUAL LIFE	COMMUNITY
COMMUNITY	SELF-DEVELOPMENT
ENVIRONMENT	HEALTH

What do the discrepancies in your two lists tell you about adjustments you need to make? What areas are deserving of more attention? If you were to live increasingly aligned with what you've decided matters most, what behaviours might you dial down or decide to drop altogether?

An awesome time

An awesome day – from the future

In this exercise, imagine you are 85. Thanks to new technology you can actually look back to any day in your life and review it. You're looking back at today and you can honestly tell yourself, *that was a really great day, I'd change nothing! I really showed up as my best self on that day.* How would you have lived today to justify such a satisfied evaluation? How did you conduct yourself? How did you treat others and yourself? What qualities did you embody? Take five minutes or longer to write down not just what you did, but how you showed up as your best self.

An awesome life – from the future

You're travelling back to the future. In this future you've had an entire life of courageous authenticity. It wasn't easy; you worked hard and showed great courage in the face of some difficult challenges. This time you are surrounded by some people who know you well. They are celebrating your awesome 85 years with you. What sort of qualities are they celebrating? What do they most appreciate about you? You're modest of course, but what sort of qualities can you justifiably be proud of having lived?

An awesome short life – from now

You've just received the diagnosis. You've got a week to live. One week! You'll feel healthy and have lots of vitality, however in seven days you'll die painlessly. How do you make the most of your week of full vitality?

What would make this one fully lived week? What will you do, what will you want to say to people, how will you engage with life?

Now repeat this exercise with periods of three months, one year and five years.

Combining your awesome life answers

Of course, you have responsibilities and finite resources. You probably are not in a position to spend the next week as if it was your last. That's not the point. The combined answers to the last few questions will tell you some important things about how to live a full and meaningful life across the shorter and longer term. Your answers can help you identify what a life of meaning *balanced across* your life span would look like. Once you know this, you can begin right away to engage with balanced meaning. There are some areas you've neglected. Begin to invest. There are some areas which have absorbed more time and energy than they merit. Dial them back.

Role models

Who do you admire? Write out a list of people you look up to. What are the qualities of each that you admire? It's okay to choose partially flawed people (because that's the only sort there are). This exercise works equally well with real people, characters from history, or fictional characters from films, Netflix or books. (Remember books?) The qualities you admire in others are likely to be qualities that would give your own life additional meaning.

Two popular strategies

Iddo Landau, Professor of Philosophy at Haifa University, Israel, and author of *Finding Meaning in an Imperfect World*, advises that there are two strategies that work for most people to increase meaning in their lives.

The first is helping others. This strategy often generates unanticipated levels of wellbeing.

The second is increasing pleasure and reducing suffering in your own life. You might think that this would be self-evident. However, modern-day busy lives can be so rushed that some people skim over the surface of their lives, never pausing to fully savour life's pleasures, small or large. The end is reached and they ask, is that it?

Enjoyment is a skill. Practise daily.

READING AND VIEWING

- Brown, Brené. *Daring Greatly: How the courage to be vulnerable transforms the way we live, love, parent and lead.* Avery, 2015.

- Brown, Brené. 'The Power of Vulnerability'. www.ted.com/talks/brene_brown_the_power_of_vulnerability.

- David, Susan. 'The Gift and Power of Emotional Courage'. www.ted.com/talks/susan_david_the_gift_and_power_of_emotional_courage.

- Hanson, Rick. 'Grow the Good that Lasts in Your Brain and Your Life'. www.rickhanson.net.

- Harris, Sam. 'Making Sense'. www.samharris.org.

- Landau, Iddo. *Finding Meaning in an Imperfect World.* Oxford University Press, 2017.

- Scapple. Literature and Latte. www.literatureandlatte.com.

CHAPTER SUMMARY

- In an authentic life we author our own lives. We take ownership.

- Your path will conflict sometimes with the expectations of others.

- Every day is packed with opportunities to boldly show up as your best self.

- Courageous authenticity is choosing and living a meaningful life with vulnerability.

- Elements of what makes your life meaningful will change over time.

- Choose what matters to you or others will choose for you.

Part IV

PLAYING TO WIN

'It is not because things are difficult that
we do not dare; it is because we do not dare
that things are difficult.'

SENECA

I'm a late convert to Netflix. Beforehand I'd been enjoying an essentially infinite collection of free online content: podcasts, videos, websites, TV. Why pay? I like free. Two of my favourite sources are TED Talks and Alain de Botton's School of Life channel on YouTube. Both are Aladdin's caves of stimulating and expertly delivered wisdom about life, delivered in delicious bite-sized pieces. I had more than enough to listen to, read and watch.

Then I broke a perfectly good right leg outdoors and was sentenced to three months of horizontality indoors. A friend nudged me towards a free introductory month of Netflix and I dived in. I was quickly hooked. I discovered the joy of ad-free binge-watching of great shows in razor-sharp definition. *Designated Survivor* starring Kiefer Sutherland is a typical example. When you get to the end of one gripping episode there's a five-second pause before it automatically starts playing the next episode. You have just five seconds to choose before you're off again. I let it roll. Again and again.

At the start of each new episode there's a recap of the story so far. You can skip it or get a quick reminder of the key things that have happened. Before we head into the next thrilling episode of this book, I'd like to offer you a quick recap of what we've covered so far. You can press SKIP, but I think it might be worthwhile.

→ SKIP INTRO

THE STORY SO FAR ...

We began with the number one regret of the dying: I wish I'd had the courage to live a life true to myself, not the life others expected of me.

Then we looked at three human predicaments that deplete courage. Firstly, a mind that's easily spooked and prioritises avoiding threats, real or imagined; secondly a culture that drip feeds us junk values and creates a trance of unworthiness; and thirdly a profound reluctance to embrace our mortality, preventing us from fully valuing our moments alive and living courageously while we can. The predicaments combine to intimidate and restrain us. As a result, at times we all live smaller, more timid and compliant lives with a defensive attitude of playing not to lose the game of life.

Rather than surrendering to our predicaments, we looked at six things we could do to embolden ourselves *prior* to meeting challenging choices. Any one of these six things could shift us from being reactive, defensive and avoidant to being proactive, courageous and towardant. Okay, I made that last word up – I mean oriented *towards* what you want more of – adopting an attitude of playing to win the game of life. Going for it, whatever 'it' means for you.

The first three emboldening strategies concern getting fit for purposeful living. How we **sleep**, **move** and **eat** each significantly impacts whether our courage batteries are charged or depleted. Bottom line, getting enough sleep, movement and good food makes being present and choiceful *much, much* easier. Easier gets my vote, and I hope it gets yours too.

Then we looked at three stances (or mindsets) that help us to play boldly throughout the days of our lives.

Defiant gratitude enriches us through appreciating what we already have, dissolving our culturally induced trance of insufficiency. Defiant gratitude for being alive now in the face of certain death soon(ish) ignites an appreciative urgency to live well now.

Self-compassion, instead of self-criticism, allows us to drop futile efforts to vanquish the fears that inevitably arise when we do what's personally important. This liberated energy can instead be redirected towards moving in meaningful directions, with fear walking (and grumbling) beside us along the way.

The third stance is one of **courageous authenticity**. Choosing what we care about and choosing to show up that way more often, even when it's challenging. We're courageously authentic when we switch from using feelings to determine what we do next, and instead choose to act like the kind of people we want to be – our best selves.

THE BEING BOLD BUFFET

I hope you'll adopt all six strategies for emboldening yourself prior to encountering challenging choices, but to be honest, one or two may be enough. Remember, we're not setting ourselves the impossible goal of being 100% authentic at all times – the perfectionist is doomed to disappointment. Success is about getting better. Living true to ourselves *more* of the time and celebrating *more* progress.

The next chapters offer three suggested approaches for taking authentic behaviour at times of challenge. You might use none, one or a combination. Entirely up to you. After all, you're choosing.

Chapter 10

THUNDERBIRDS ARE GO!

'It is easier to act yourself into a new way of thinking,
than it is to think yourself into a new way of acting.'

MILLARD FULLER

This is going to date me, but to hell with it. I grew up watching the original *Thunderbirds* show on TV, and it was awesome. The fantastic premise was this: in the late 21st century ex-astronaut Jeff Tracy uses his personal fortune to buy a palm-fringed pacific island, build a luxurious home and establish International Rescue, a private emergency response service. He has five high-tech rescue craft, the Thunderbirds, and each one is piloted by a family member. My favourite was Thunderbird One, a reusable SpaceX-style rocket. Prior to launch, the swimming pool would slide to one side to allow the rocket to take off from a secret launchpad beneath. Brilliant! I don't have a pool, but if I did, it wouldn't be complete without a rocket underneath.

Every episode started dramatically as a deep American voice counted down the launch of Thunderbird One: 'Five. Four. Three. Two. One ... ' Then a launch scene with plenty of smoke ... 'Thunderbirds are go!' Thrilling stuff, and with stirring theme music to boot. (YouTube link on the next page.)

In her book *The 5 Second Rule*, motivational speaker Mel Robbins describes how she had been going through a rough patch in life. Finding the motivation to even get out of bed was a struggle, never mind confronting life's other challenges. Then she saw a space shuttle launch on TV. She saw the familiar shape of the shuttle on the launchpad, heard a voice count down from five to one, and saw the rockets fire. The shuttle was up and away! She resolved to start her next day with a countdown before launching herself into action.

It worked. When the time to get up arrived she counted herself down. She got up. She got going.

As she went through her day, she noticed that when she thought about doing something challenging but worthwhile her brain would stop her by generating doubt, worry, excuses or fear. To interrupt her fearful brain she started experimenting by counting down from five to one and taking action. It worked again.

Here's how Mel describes her 5 Second Rule: 'The moment you have an instinct to act on a goal you must 5–4–3–2–1 and physically move or your brain will stop you.'

Sometimes, all of us know exactly what we need to do ... but heck, we just don't feel like it. It could be speaking up in a meeting, going to the gym, talking to someone new, asking for help or applying for a new job. A countdown followed by a launch is sometimes all it takes to focus the mind and activate your courageous self.

Occasionally, when I have something challenging to do I'll say the Thunderbirds countdown in my head: 'Five. Four. Three. Two. One. Thunderbirds are go!' And I'm off again on my next adventure.

I know it's a bit silly, but hey, if it works, why not? Next time you're procrastinating, try out the 5 Second Rule. It just might do the trick.

READING AND VIEWING

- Network Distributing. *Thunderbirds: HD Restored Title Sequence.* www.youtube.com/watch?v=3HWhEikJmIM.

- Robbins, Mel. *The 5 Second Rule: Transform your life, work, and confidence with everyday courage.* Savio Republic, 2017.

CHAPTER SUMMARY

- When it's time to act like your best self, 5-4-3-2-1 and launch into action.

Chapter 11

UPGRADE YOUR SELF-IMAGE

'Life isn't about finding yourself.
Life is about creating yourself.'

ANONYMOUS

Getting picked last for a school sports team can be pretty dispiriting. I should know. Football, hockey, or cricket, I sucked at them all. I was slow, uncoordinated and unsure of the rules. Every game was an opportunity to demonstrate my athletic inadequacies. But I wasn't alone. Three of us were equally talent-lite on the sports field, Craig, Daniel and myself. We were The Three Liabilities. On a good sports day, a really good one, I'd be selected third or second to last. I had escaped the conspicuous humiliation of being the least wanted player.

ZERO TO HERO

A small Texan boy called Lanny Bassham was also terrible at sports at school. He was mostly kept off the baseball field, and when allowed on he'd be sent to the spot where he could do the least harm. His sports ability was so unremittingly dreadful that he was singled out in class as being least likely to succeed at an Olympics. Lanny might have made a great Fourth Liability, but he has since proved himself ineligible. As Wikipedia tells us, Lanny went on to 'win three gold medals at the Pan American Games, three Individual World Titles at the World Shooting Championships in 1974, World Champion in 50m three-position in the 1978 World shooting Championships, and a total of 22 world individual and team titles, setting four world records. At the 1974 World Shooting Championships in Switzerland Lanny won 15 medals, the most any individual athlete has ever won in a single World Shooting Championships.' Oh, and he also won gold at the 1976 Montreal Olympics.

How did he pull it off? Lanny describes his zero-to-hero transformation in his book *With Winning in Mind*. He explains how each of us tends to behave like the kind of person we think we are. And this applies in sports, at work and at home.

If you think of yourself as trustworthy, you'll keep promises.

If you think of yourself as a healthy eater, you'll make healthy food choices.

If you think of yourself as dependable, you'll show up when you said you would.

If, on the other hand, you think of yourself as lazy, no good on dates, or unable to resist a drink, then lo and behold, you probably will be. Our self-image often acts as a self-fulfilling prophecy. We realise our expectations.

SELF-IMAGE - CARVED FROM EXPERIENCE

Far from being fixed, your self-image or identity is something that evolves over your life. It's shaped by the experiences you have and what you notice about yourself. It's almost as if your mind is continually looking for evidence about the kind of person you are. It's noticing what sort of things you do and the results you get. Single events don't count for much, but repetition is more convincing.

Lanny puts his extraordinary success down in large part to his techniques for adjusting how he thought about himself. He resolved to craft a self-image of being a world-class shooter. As a result, he became one. Shooting with excellence was now simply who he was.

Some of you may be wondering if he achieved this by chanting positive affirmations in front of the mirror every morning. Nope. This may be a popular self-help approach among the well-meaning, but sadly, the evidence is that it only works if you already believe what you're saying. Lanny had a much better way of improving performance in sports, work and life, a method he calls the Mind Management System. He's taught this to US Navy SEALs, SWAT teams, CEOs, PGA Tour golfers and the FBI.

Lanny knew that the human mind has a tendency, if left to itself, to ruminate over mistakes and spend only brief moments enjoying successes. As a result, most people spend a lot of time remembering and reliving errors in their minds. They mentally practise poor performance and accidentally reinforce a self-image of someone who screws up. He figured that he would flip this around. From now on, he would intentionally focus on what went well, and skip over errors. Athletes refer to this as 'feast and forget', where great results are relished and poor performance is given minimal mind time.

Whenever Lanny got excellent results while shooting, he would pause afterwards, savour the experience and tell himself *that's like me!* His own mind heard the words, looked at the evidence, and had to agree. It *was* just like him.

However, he didn't just wait for great results in the real world. He rehearsed them too. Lanny says he won his Olympic gold medal over a thousand times in his mind before competing in Montreal in 1976. He didn't rehearse stepping up to the podium and enjoying the roar of the crowd. No, what he imagined daily and repeatedly was the action of shooting *really* well. Getting in position, the breathing, focusing, and squeezing of the trigger – seeing the target shot perfectly. This repeated experience of excellence gradually etched a self-image of excellence into his mind.

The mind isn't that good at distinguishing what's real from what's fantasy. Imagine opening a fridge door right now and seeing a lemon inside. You know what lemons look like – this one's especially large and a vivid yellow. Picking it up you notice the cold sensations of its firm, waxy skin. Putting that lemon on a wooden chopping board, you easily slice it in half with a sharp knife, a few drops of lemon juice dripping onto the board. Reaching out to pick up one half of the lemon, you raise it slowly to your mouth. Squeezing it, you feel the cold juice run into your mouth and onto your chin. Cold, wet lemon juice. All over your tongue.

Just writing this makes my mouth water. For something that isn't there.

The mind responds to vividly imagined experiences in a similar way to actual ones. Lanny utilised this to give himself as many experiences of success as he could, both real *and* imagined. He had a three-step strategy and made it a habit:

1. Before taking a shot, he would imagine experiencing success, as vividly as he could.

2. When he took a shot, if he was successful he would pause to relish it and tell himself, *that's like me!* If he was unsuccessful he just moved on.

3. After practice, he filled out a performance journal in which he described his best shots. He relived them again in his mind, tasting excellence.

Of course, there's nothing more vivid than real life, so real beats imaginary. He practised on the range a great deal. However, when he didn't have an opportunity to practise for real, Lanny practised in his head. In this way he never missed a day's practice. His self-image was adjusted over time through multiple experiences, real and imagined. And as his self-image improved, his performance followed. He became his best self.

OLYMPIC TRAINING

Mental rehearsal is now common in many Olympic disciplines, from bobsledding, snowboarding and diving to fencing, gymnastics and judo. Kayla Harrison, World Judo Championship winner and winner of gold at both the London 2012 and Rio 2016 Olympics, uses mental imagery extensively. In the years running up to both events, she rehearsed successful performance every night just before falling asleep. When she wakes up on competition day, she says her body just knows what to do: *It's time. This is it. Like I've been there a thousand times.* As a result, she finds herself showing up as her best self.

Most of us won't be awarded a gold medal for showing up as our best selves. But how we choose to talk to ourselves after authentic action will influence whether we do it again.

MIND YOUR LANGUAGE

Some folk unwittingly undermine their self-image by the thoughts they have right after taking successful action. I certainly used to do this. Let's say you've resolved to be someone who does something worthwhile but difficult, like eating a salad when you felt like chips, or going for a walk when you felt like slouching on the sofa. Right after finishing you might tell yourself something along the lines of, *Done it – I've been good!* When you tell yourself *I've been good!*, what you're telling yourself is, *I was good that time. That's not really like me.* Uh oh. And when your mind hears you've been good, it gives you what psychologists call 'moral credit'. Moral credit gives you a pass for poor behaviour. You deserve those chips and a good sofa slouch. You've earnt it.

> 'The wise man does nothing unwillingly.'
>
> **SENECA**

The way to avoid this pitfall is as follows. Before starting, consciously choose to do the difficult thing willingly. You don't *have* to do this thing – you're choosing to because of your own reasons: *I'm having the salad because I want to be healthy for my family* or *I'm going for a run because I want the energy to be a great dad.* Once you've completed the demanding task, pause to savour your achievement and feel free to tell yourself, *that's like me!* If that expression doesn't work for you, try *that's the kind of person I'm becoming.*

THE AUTHENTICITY HABIT

James Clear, author of *Atomic Habits*, writes that 'every action you take is a vote for the type of person you wish to become'. Our self-image is evolving daily through real and imagined actions. When we recognise this, we discover a way to take more control over the directions our lives take. We can choose to establish the habits that will develop us daily into the kind of people we most want to be. It's less important where you are today. What matters more is your trajectory.

Is your best self a loving parent? What sort of things would a loving parent do daily? Make it a habit.

Is your best self a skillful artist? What sort of things would a skillful artist do daily? Make it a habit.

Is your best self healthy, fit and vital? What sort of things does a healthy, fit and vital person do daily? Make it a habit.

Habits do require effort to set up. You'll need to actively choose to swipe right on your best self. Once established, they run themselves, reinforcing your self-image daily. I can highly recommend *Atomic Habits* to anyone interested in improving the quality of their lives through implementing habits aligned with the kind of person you're choosing to be. When we do this, we're not waiting for others to pick us to join their team. We're picking ourselves.

READING

- Basham, Lanny. *With Winning in Mind* 3rd Edition. Mental Management Systems, 2012.

- Clear, James. *Atomic Habits: An easy and proven way to build good habits & break bad ones.* New York: Avery, 2018.

- Maese, Rick. *'For Olympians, Seeing (In Their Minds) is Believing (It Can Happen)'.* 28 July 2016. www.washingtonpost.com/sports/olympics/for-olympians-seeing-in-their-minds-is-believing-it-can-happen/2016/07/28/6966709c-532e-11e6-bbf5-957ad17b4385_story.html.

CHAPTER SUMMARY

- We behave like the kind of people we think we are.

- Self-image is shaped by experience.

- Feast on experiences, real and imagined, that build your best self-image.

- Establish habits of action that are aligned with the kind of person you are choosing to become.

Chapter 12

SWIPE RIGHT IN SEVEN STEPS

'The art of being yourself at your best
is the art of unfolding yourself into the
personality you want to be.'

WILFRED PETERSON

In this chapter I'll share an emotionally intelligent way to show up as your best self when challenged. The seven steps are based on principles of human behaviour proven to help people improve their performance – at work, in sports, in health, in taking care of yourself and taking care of others. This approach applies any time you need to do something personally worthwhile and personally challenging. Which I reckon applies to pretty much every day well spent.

THE SWIPE RIGHT MODEL

Here's a map of the seven steps. The first four are preparation for playing your best game. The last three steps are how to effectively tackle challenges in the game itself.

Hat tip and deep bow of humility to the numerous awesome researchers, teachers, practitioners and writers whose ideas shape this model. Special call out to Steven Hayes, professor of psychology at the University of Nevada, Reno. Steven is one of the most cited psychologists in the world and has authored over 600 scientific articles and 43 books. He initiated the development of Acceptance and Commitment Therapy (ACT), a proven approach to improving the ability to meet life's challenges courageously. A real giant in the world of human behaviour whose work has transformed human wellbeing and performance globally. Thanks also to Benji Schoendorff and Kevin Polk, authors of *The Essential ACT Matrix*, for the first four steps, and Jon Hill and Joe Oliver, authors of *Acceptance and Commitment Coaching*, for the last three steps.

The Swipe Right Model

IMPORTANCE   FEARS   NOTICE   NOW WHAT?

TOWARDS MOVES   AWAY MOVES   NAME

Before we step through the model, we need to select a challenge to apply it to.

Pick a challenge

The seven steps are used to meet challenges well. As a human being with a pulse, I'm confident your day already includes multiple challenges. Or perhaps you would like to boldly set yourself a new one? Which challenge are you willing to work on, and unwilling to postpone? It could be related to work, health, relationships, study, sport – any area that *you* care about. Pick something important now.

The area I'm going to work on is:

_____

_____

_____

Now it's time to get specific. If you were to get better at doing *just one thing*, which one thing would make the biggest difference? Here are some examples:

- For a health goal, maybe you want to get better at drinking less alcohol or coffee. Exercise more or adjust your diet. Maybe improve the hours and quality of sleep.

- At work you might want to respond more constructively to a challenging co-worker. Or delegate more effectively. Improve your listening skills. Maybe pause more often before acting.

- In your relationships you might want to get better at listening and not telling. Understanding and not fixing. Dialling down criticism and dialling up hearing. I'm just saying! None of this applies to me of course (cough).

You get the idea. The important thing is you choose an improvement goal that matters to you. It might also matter to someone else, but it needs to matter to you more. It's an improvement goal that is authentic – it represents the kind of person you want to be. It mustn't be about improving somebody else (regardless of how much you know they need upgrading) – it needs to be your own personal development goal.

My improvement goal for this area is to get better at:

_____

_____

_____

_____

Great – now you've got something specific to work on. Before launching into the Swipe Right Model, you'll need a blank Swipe Right Matrix to write on, like the one below. You can get a copy of this form from www.ericwinters.com.au/swiperight-exercises. Or simply grab a blank sheet of paper and draw four lines on it and two arrows. Funky icons are entirely optional!

The Swipe Right Matrix

AWAY MOVES

TOWARDS MOVES

FEARS

IMPORTANCE

As you're about to discover, the right side shows your courageous best self. The you that moves towards what you care about. This is who you're going to swipe right on.

The left side shows your defensive self. The you who moves away from vulnerability. This is the self you're going to be kind to.

Okay, it's time to begin with an honest inventory. Let's look at the first four steps.

1. Importance

What's important about your improvement goal? Why does this really matter to you? Write your answer in the bottom-right matrix quadrant.

2. Towards moves

What specifically would your best self do to move towards what's important, even when you're feeling challenged? Write specific visible actions in the top-right matrix quadrant.

3. Fears

What shows up sometimes that gets in the way of you being your best self? Write down any uncomfortable thoughts and feelings that arise in the bottom left.

4. Away moves

What can you be seen doing to move away from what's below? In other words, what do you sometimes do to make yourself feel better?

Let's look at some examples on the following pages.

Example 1

Area: Work

Improvement goal: To get better at delegating

AWAY MOVES   TOWARDS MOVES

AWAY MOVES

- Do it all myself
- Reject offers to help
- Micromanage

TOWARDS MOVES

- Delegate small tasks
- Provide task clarity
- Provide support
- Request progress updates

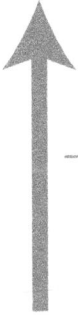

FEARS

- They'll screw it up!
- They'll take too long
- I'm the only one who can do it right

IMPORTANCE

- Being an effective leader
- Developing my leadership
- Developing my team
- Freeing up my time
- Utilising the team's talent

FEARS   IMPORTANCE

Example 2

Area: Health

Improvement goal: To get better at living alcohol-free

AWAY MOVES   TOWARDS MOVES

AWAY MOVES

- Buy alcohol on drive home
- Have a glass when I get home
- Keep alcohol at home
- Drink after work
- Drink at lunch

TOWARDS MOVES

- Celebrate progress
- Keep an alcohol-free home
- Choose alternative alcohol-free drinks
- Look at family photo when I feel urge

FEARS

- Not drinking is unbearable
- The urge to drink will last all night
- I can't enjoy myself without alcohol
- Friends will disapprove

IMPORTANCE

- Greater energy for work and life
- Be a good role model for my kids
- Fit into more of my clothes
- Being the best partner I can be
- Enjoy workdays more
- Be fit for life and love

FEARS   IMPORTANCE

144

Example 3

Area: Relationships

Improvement goal: To get better at listening to my partner

AWAY MOVES TOWARDS MOVES

AWAY MOVES

- Tell my partner what they should do
- Suggesting solutions when not asked
- Changing the topic
- Talking about myself

TOWARDS MOVES

- Pausing before responding
- Asking what happened
- Asking what that was like
- Asking what else
- Checking my understanding
- Letting them know I get them

FEARS

- If I don't tell them what I think right away then I'm unhelpful
- If I do listen then it will take too long and be a waste of time

IMPORTANCE

- Loving my partner
- Being supportive
- Improving all my relationships

FEARS IMPORTANCE

SWIPING RIGHT

Now that we've prepared our Swipe Right Matrix, we know what's been getting in the way and how we would like to show up instead. We can choose our best self at the time of challenge in three steps.

5. Notice

Thanks to the matrix you've completed, you have an idea what kinds of thoughts and feelings to expect when you're challenged. The first step to interrupting avoidance behaviours is to actually notice what shows up, *as* it shows up. When challenges do arise, pause and direct your attention *with kindness* to whatever you're feeling or telling yourself. A friendly attitude to your experience is key.

6. Name

Name that thought or feeling and do this with friendliness. When we name it, we tame it, but only if we're kind.

Ahh, I'm having the thought that I'm not good enough.

Ahh, I'm telling myself the 'this will never work' story.

Ahh, there's fear.

Ahh, there's stress.

For a terrific list of ways of doing this step, take a look at *The Happiness Trap Pocketbook* by Russ Harris. It's so good I often give a copy to my coaching clients.

7. Now what?

Now what would the person you want to be do? You've already written this in your matrix. Do that! You'll notice the icon above shows a heroic figure with a symbol of fear on their cape. This is to remind us that courage is taking action in the presence of fear, in the service of what we care about.

At this step, you could also 5–4–3–2–1 and launch yourself into action. Thunderbirds are go!

FINAL THOUGHTS

The first Swipe Right Matrix you create is just a draft to get you going. You update it with experience. You might find that the fears you thought you had aren't actually the ones showing up at all. Or you might discover additional things that make this improvement goal important. The matrix is always a work in progress. You refine it over time as you build self-awareness.

The final three steps in which you swipe right on your best self are skills. They are things you'll get better at. Enjoy the progress. That's like you!

More final thoughts

To get really good at using this model, I strongly recommend teaming up with a coach experienced in using ACT. They're sometimes called an 'acceptance and commitment coach'. You might attend a workshop or get a few private sessions face to face or over the phone. They'll help you get better at taking each of the seven steps.

Organisations large and small around the world also use the principles I've outlined to help leaders, teams and organisations to work together more effectively. The research shows that when people learn these skills, either in a single day workshop or more typically in several brief sessions over a few weeks, then good things follow. People experience greater wellbeing, performance improves, they apply what they learn in other training better and they manage change more effectively. If your workplace might benefit from a skills training program like this, conducted on-site or virtually, feel free to email me at hello@ericwinters.com.au.

READING

- Harris, Russ. *The Happiness Trap Pocketbook: An illustrated guide on how to stop struggling and start living.* Constable and Robinson, 2014.

- Hill, Jon, and Oliver, Joe. *Acceptance and Commitment Coaching: Distinctive features.* Routledge, 2019.

- Polk, Kevin L., Schoendorff, Benjamin; Webster, Mark and Olaz, Fabian. *The Essential Guide to the ACT Matrix: A step-by-step approach to using the ACT matrix model in clinical practice.* Context Press, 2016.

CHAPTER SUMMARY

Choosing to make courageous decisions is a skill. It's something we can get better at, individually and in teams. The seven-step Swipe Right Model has been developed to help us do just that.

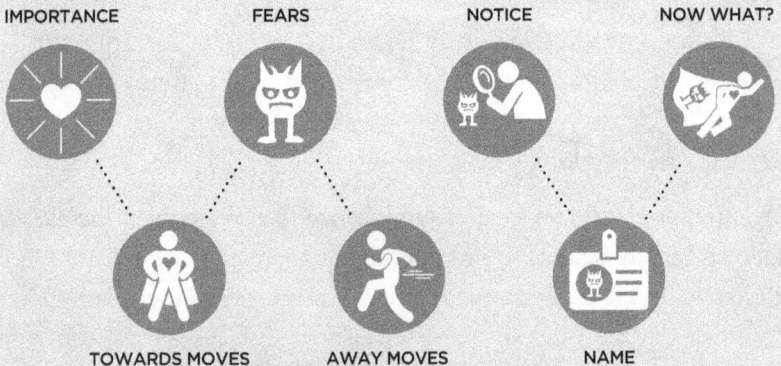

IMPORTANCE   FEARS   NOTICE   NOW WHAT?

TOWARDS MOVES   AWAY MOVES   NAME

CONCLUSION

'Success is not final, failure is not fatal.
It is the courage to continue that counts.'

WINSTON CHURCHILL

Each year on 26 December, about 100 yachts set off from Sydney Harbour in one of the world's most challenging events, the Sydney to Hobart Yacht Race. Crafts of all shapes and sizes brave the 1170 kilometre route across the Tasman Sea and Bass Strait, waters renowned for high winds and difficult conditions. Tragedy struck in 1998 when hurricane-strength winds sank five boats and six people died. Of the 115 boats that started, only 44 made it to Hobart.

Although there's considerable interest in which yacht arrives first in Hobart, there's also a handicap race which rewards the craft that sailed the most effectively, taking into account size and other characteristics. Since the race began in 1945, the handicap winner has been the fastest craft only seven times.

Each crew member lucky enough to participate is deeply committed to sailing as effectively as possibly. The yachts are lovingly maintained prior to the race to be optimally fit for purpose. The crew members train their bodies and build the resilient mindsets necessary to meet the challenges ahead. They can't control the weather, but they can control how they skilfully sail within the weather they're given. They control how they show up within the predicaments in which they find themselves.

It matters. Lives are at stake.

In the preceding chapters we've looked at some of the predicaments we find ourselves in on our own challenging voyages through life. To optimise our own courageous adventuring we considered three ways we could prepare our craft to be fit for purpose, three stances to provide strong foundations for bold performance, and three strategies to help us to do what's personally important and challenging. Because it matters. The quality of our lives is at stake.

Every new unlived moment of each day provides a fresh opportunity to swipe right on your best self. To courageously choose to live a life true to yourself. Daring to initiate, to love, to learn and to lead yourself and others through this impossibly precious life. With gratitude, compassion and authenticity.

Leading such a life isn't only personally rewarding. The challenges facing our communities, workplaces and environment demand courageous thinking, collaboration and action if we're going to meet them effectively. We need each other to live courageously.

Thunderbirds are go!

I'd be thrilled to hear how you apply the ideas in this book as you courageously have the adventure of *your* life. What made the most positive impact to your professional or personal life? Email me at hello@ericwinters.com.au.

WORKING WITH ERIC

If you've enjoyed reading *Swipe Right on Your Best Self* then you may be interested in finding out more about building courageous authenticity.

Eric helps leaders build skills for meeting challenges effectively *and* realising personal ambitions through a range of coaching programmes, impactful workshops and inspiring keynotes. These are available virtually and in person.

As you'll be well aware, the challenge of change is picking up pace in many areas: health, the climate, the economy, in business, financial, technological and social domains, to name just a few.

Professional or personal, global or local, meeting challenges well requires courage.

The courage to challenge redundant approaches to living and working.

The courage to have the conversations that have been avoided.

The courage to bring more of ourselves into work and life.

The courage to share our ideas and thinking.

The courage to listen to others and ourselves.

The courage to initiate, fail, learn and re-learn.

The courage to boldly voice new ways of working and living with each other on this one precious planet.

You can find out more about working with Eric at:

His website: ericwinters.com.au

On LinkedIn: linkedin.com/in/ericwinterscomau

On Facebook: facebook.com/ericwinterscomau

As a reader who made it all the way through, you are also invited to share stories of how you use the ideas in this book to positively impact your own courageous life. Your experience will inspire others.

You can contact Eric at hello@ericwinters.com.au. He'd love to hear from you.

ERIC⦿WINTERS
SELF-LEADERSHIP SPEAKER • AUTHOR • COACH

www.ingramcontent.com/pod-product-compliance
Lightning Source LLC
Chambersburg PA
CBHW071642210326
41597CB00017B/2087